Valentino Forever

THE HISTORY OF THE VALENTINO MEMORIAL SERVICES

By

Tracy Ryan Terhune

First published by AuthorHouse 06/23/04

ISBN: 1-4184-0523-X (e-book)
ISBN: 1-4184-0522-1 (Paperback)

Library of Congress Control Number: 2004090489

This book is printed on acid free paper.

Printed in the United States of America
Bloomington, IN

Dedicated to the Memory of
Rudolph Valentino
May You Be Remembered
Forever

Introduction

In August 1926 the world responded to the untimely death of the thirty-one year old silent screen actor Rudolph Valentino with shock, disbelief and an enormous outpouring of emotion that had been prodded by sensational tabloid newspaper headlines. The tens of thousands in the crowd cramming the streets during Valentino's lying-in-state at Campbell's Funeral Church on Manhattan's west side became so unruly that plate glass store windows were shattered, cars overturned, and mounted police had to be summoned to the scene. Women fainted and several suicides, said to be prompted by Valentino's death, were reported. At the two Valentino funerals that followed, one on August 30th at St Malachy's Church in New York and a second on September 7th in the Beverly Hills Church of the Good Shepherd, the throngs that gathered to pay their last respects were far more subdued than those in front of Campbell's, but full of grief. Such sustained demonstrations of mourning on behalf of a screen actor were unprecedented, and served as a testament not just to Rudolph Valentino's special place in the affections of everyday people but also to the extraordinary influence motion pictures had come to exert during the American 1920s.

Tracy Terhune, a long time Valentino aficionado and collector who heads the Yahoo Valentino e-group, knows perhaps better than anyone else that as one Valentino saga came to a tragic end on August 23, 1926 with the Italian-born actor's passing, another soon began in its wake: the tradition of commemorating the anniversary of Valentino's death with a memorial service conducted each year at 12:10 pm in the place of his interment, the Cathedral Mausoleum at the Santa Monica Boulevard cemetery that used to be called Hollywood Memorial and is now known as Hollywood Forever.

Every year since 1927 some sort of Valentino memorial service has taken place, and in all but one instance that event was held in the mausoleum where the remains of Valentino rest in the June Mathis family crypt. For more than seventy five years, the custom of ritualized tribute and commemoration, involving song, prayer, recollections, poetry and floral offerings, has developed and been sustained. That tradition is the subject of *VALENTINO FOREVER.*

Tracy Terhune's research benefits from his own thoroughness and dedication as well as that of the other collectors, who provided him full access to their treasured documents and photographs. A cast of colorful characters, the habitual attendees of the memorials, emerges on these pages, including several rival claimants to the title, The Lady in Black. More than any other, Ditra Flame, the first, most devoted and most long-tenured Lady in Black, commands the spotlight, for she documented many early memorials and left scrapbooks filled with her clipping collection and correspondence. She competed, in time, with two rival claimants to the title of the Lady in Black, one-time Ziegfeld Follies beauty Marion Benda, who had actually dated Valentino shortly before he died, and drama queen Estrellita del Regil. At times the competition between Ditra Flame and Estrellita Del Regil, a fixture of the services in the 70s and 80s, takes on a MOMMIE DEAREST aspect, as hissy fits are thrown and the roses deposited in the crypt's urns by one Lady are replaced by white daisies or thrown to the ground and stomped upon by the other. The Los Angeles press habitually paid far more attention to the various Ladies in Black than they did to the departed Valentino. They provided better photo-ops.

If in past decades the doings of a parade of "second rate talent, publicity seekers, fringe showbiz characters, crackpots and faux mourners" produced a carnival atmosphere that enraged Valentino's brother Alberto and nephew Jean, the memorials in recent years often possess the poignancy that comes with deep feeling and true respect. So many movie fans continue to be moved by, and to care about, Rudolph Valentino. The former silent players such as James Kirkwood and Mary MacLaren who used to be regular participants, and the Hollywood historians who stand in for them nowadays, participated in the memorials out of a wish to honor not just Rudolph Valentino, but the glory days of early Hollywood.

If this saga has a hero, he is Tyler Cassity, since 1998 the owner (with his brother) of Hollywood Forever, who restored the buildings and grounds from the deterioration and neglect they had suffered and brought new dignity and thoughtful planning to the memorials. Tracy Terhune honors him here as he narrates a chapter of Hollywood history never told before, and very much worth telling.

Emily W. Leider

San Francisco, October 2003

Acknowledgements

I am deeply indebted to many people who generously opened their private collections without conditions or restrictions. They believed in this project and supported me wholeheartedly every step of the way.

Emily Leider, author of the critically acclaimed Valentino biography *Dark Lover*, was one of the very first to encourage me to write this story. Long before her own book had been printed; she took the time to encourage me to pursue my idea. It's my honor to have a Valentino authority of her stature write the introduction to *Valentino Forever*. I am most appreciative of her kindness and support (and numerous helpful suggestions). Also, my personal thanks to her husband, Bill Leider.

Michael and Virginia Back welcomed me with open arms into their home on numerous occasions, often with my computer in tow, to peruse through their unequalled Valentino collection of almost 60 years. Almost all of the vintage 1920's – 1950's photographs you will enjoy in this book are courtesy of their generosity. I am doubly proud to know them not only in my capacity as author of this book, but as my close friends.

Jim Craig had the great foresight to acquire and preserve Ditra Flame's unbelievable lifetime collection – items that included her personal scrapbook, diary, numerous photos, newspaper clippings as well as several hundred letters of her private correspondence. All of it pertains to the Valentino Memorial Service. Jim offered me unlimited access to these materials and later allowed me to purchase them outright. Jim did retain Ditra's treasured black veil!

Thanks also go to my friend Donna Hill, a much respected Valentino authority who helped me immensely by providing digital screen grabs from new and old video to fill in gaps where no physical photos were to be had. A valued contributor to *Valentino Forever*, via writing the epilogue. Always with encouragement, she made available any and all Valentino Memorial related photographs and materials from her vast Valentino collection to be shared here.

Steve Sanders is to be thanked over and over for taking on the dubious task of reviewing and editing this book. He spent untold hours correcting my spelling and sentence structures, offering alternative ways to say the same thing, only better. As the author of best selling books *Desilu* and the equally successful *Rainbow's End*, his valuable input put the polish on this book.

Thomas Blount, owner of Valentino's home Falcon Lair has graciously invited me to the residence on numerous occasions, and gifted me with some prized Valentino treasures. His kindness is very much appreciated.

To my co-workers at Universal Studios all who were just as eager as I was in seeing this project completed; I offer my thanks for their support and enthusiasm. Todd Riley, Vicki Barton, Naira Avetisyan, Iris Tran, Kim Meyer, Martell Webster and Chad Anselmo.

Others that assisted me includes my life-long friend Tammie Kadin who has come to join me in going to the Valentino Memorial as an annual tradition of her own. Valentino Memorial veteran Stella Grace - who always encouraged me via our many long distance phone calls and is my close personal friend, whose advise I value. A big thanks goes to John Hillman (Silent Cinema) for the loan of his Valentino photos.

A huge thank you to Mike McKelvy who helped me by providing many photographs and documents from his files on Bud Testa, Mary MacLaren, Mary Philbin and Estrellita. His assistance was instrumental to this book. Thanks and a high-five goes to Woolsey Ackerman, Frank Labrador, Armando Rueda, Tommy Armstrong, Ray Hernandez, Mario Lizarraga, Sebastian Lupercio, George Dalzell,

John Sampson, Max Hoffman, Rock Armstrong, Melissa Delgado, Rudy Freeman, Dave R. Smith.

Thanks to all the members of the Yahoo! "We Never Forget" Valentino e-group for keeping the discussion going day after day. Appreciation and my respect goes to Allan Ellenberger for his keen research and generosity in sharing information, ideas and materials, even as he is working on a Valentino book project of his own at the same time.

Thanks to Hollywood Forever Cemetery for many kindnesses not only towards me and this book, but for continuing to be supportive of the Valentino Memorial Service.

For recognizing the importance of the Valentino Memorial Service, and its significance as one of the oldest continuing Hollywood traditions, very special thanks go to Tyler Cassity. Also my thanks to Deborah "Bee" MacRae who is always radiant and helpful.

Thanks to my parents Bob Terhune and especially my mother, Lila Terhune who spent time with me discussing her book ideas as well as the publishing process.

Also recognition of friends and family who aren't here to share in this project. My Aunt Maxine Wright, John Ortega, Scotty McGlynn, and my best friend whom I miss so much, Alex Logan.

Thanks everyone! I couldn't have done it without you.

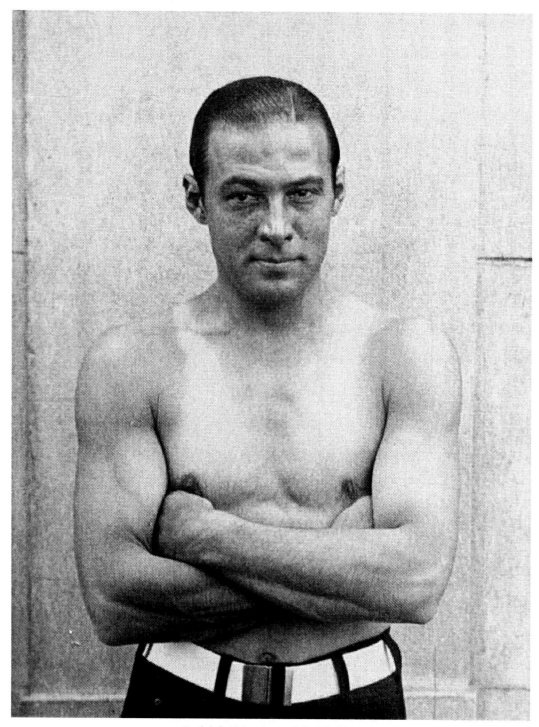

Rudolph Valentino – July 23, 1926

Foreword

July 23, 1926. Exactly one month after this image was captured on film Rudolph Valentino would be dead. No one imagined that fateful day in August would become ingrained in Hollywood tradition. Never to be forgotten. Never. Indeed, for the first time in motion picture history, all movie studios in Hollywood stopped production for two full minutes, solely in his memory. It was destined to become a date which the faithful would duly note on their calendars, year after year. All for the sake of making a pilgrimage to his crypt at Hollywood Memorial Cemetery.

Hollywood had never witnessed anything equal to it. Although Hollywood's movie industry was still in its infancy, Rudolph Valentino's peers were astonished to hear the news that over 10,000 people had rioted in New York, smashing plate glass windows, pushing, shoving, trampling each other, fainting and collapsing, fighting and skirmishing with the police. All for just a fleeting two-second parting glimpse of his body. An estimated 100,000 people passed by his bier each day it was on view. As for seeing their idol, Rudolph Valentino in the flesh, as quoted in the silent film documentary *Hollywood*, "for some it was the first, for all, the last."

At 10:00 a.m. final services were held for Valentino in Beverly Hills at the Church of the Good Shepherd on September 7, 1926 Admittance was by invitation only. The casket was met at the doorway by Father Michael J. Mullins, who blessed it with Holy Water while it slowly proceeded to the front of the church. Accepting the title of honorary pall bearers were Cecil B. DeMille, Douglas Fairbanks, Samual Goldwyn, Jesse L. Lasky, William S. Hart, Mack Sennett, Louis B. Mayer and Hal Roach. Active pallbearers, who carried the casket were Charlie Chaplin, John W. Considine, Jr., Mario Carrillo, George Fitzmaurice, Emmett Flynn, Count Gradenigo, and Tullio Carminatti. Official ushers for the service were Antonio Moreno, Lon Chaney, John Gilbert, George O'Brien, and Malcolm McGregor. A virtual who's who of 1920's Hollywood elite were present. This included former wife Jean Acker and Pola Negri, Mary Pickford, Douglas Fairbanks, John Gilbert, William S. Hart, Antonio Moreno, Mr. and Mrs. Ernst Lubitsch, Mabel Normand, Harold Lloyd, Estelle Taylor, Elinor Glyn, Samuel Goldwyn, Jesse Lasky, June Mathis, Agnes Ayres, Marion Davies, Mr. and Mrs. S. George Ullman. Norman Kerry who had been selected as a pallbearer had to decline due to an ankle broken the day before, and arrived at the church leaning on crutches. Also attending was Valentino's trusted handyman and the man who Rudolph chose as a witness signature on his last will and testament, Luther Mahoney.

With everyone standing at the conclusion of the brief mass, the casket was carried out of the church, from the balcony the chapel was filled with the rich voice of Chicago Grand Opera baritone star, Richard Bonnelli, who tenderly sang a heart-wrenching version of *Ave Maria.* Hardened studio executives and family alike were moved to tears.

Leaving the church, the hearse solemnly made its way down Santa Monica Blvd. Extensive crowds lined both sides of the streets. Equally, both men and women. All were genuinely saddened. Their only wish was to be afforded this last opportunity to not only witness history, but to express their deep loss and silently offer their sincere respect.

The funeral procession was on its last journey. The final destination was 6000 Santa Monica Boulevard: Hollywood Memorial Park Cemetery. As the hearse and funeral procession passed within the entrance gates of the cemetery, the roar of a low flying plane could be heard. All eyes were cast skyward as the throng witnessed an occupant in the plane dramatically scattering fresh roses in front of the path of the funeral procession. Within moments a second plane joined the first in scattering the scented roses. This tribute was thought of, and paid for by Luther Mahoney. A rain of roses from heaven, which by self-admission was Rudy's favorite flower. A last sincere gesture for a dear, beloved friend.

Once the casket was carried down the marble halls, it was placed within the niche that was originally intended for June Mathis. The only persons allowed within the mausoleum were the pallbearers, Father Michael J. Mullins, and Valentino's brother Alberto Valentino, S. George Ullman and Pola Negri. A last prayer was offered, and incredibly, the bronze casket was raised into the niche and sealed. Among Pola's tears, the solemn ceremonies concluded.

Since that fateful day, September 7, 1926, when the mortal remains of Rudolph Valentino were interred, until now, almost eight decades later, hundreds upon thousands have journeyed from all parts of the world to visit his grave. Many choose to go quietly and simply leave flowers. Some come at various times of the year, such as his birthday on May 6th, or on Christmas, New Years, Memorial Day, or any given holiday.

It is not uncommon to randomly visit the grave any day of the year and see a wineglass, half filled with vintage Italian wine, with an attached note toasting him for his lasting contribution. To see Christmas cards, birthday cards, Holy Bible's, personal heartfelt notes, inspirational poems, and even lipstick marks upon the marble face of his crypt, and various other expressions, in an attempt to let him know, somehow, some way, that he is still in their hearts.

Starting in 1927 and continuing until this very year, an annual memorial service has been conducted without interruption. In 1928 the cemetery announced that within the first two years of his death, an estimated 100,000 people had visited his crypt. The names and the "players" have changed, as time has marched on. But the brilliant endurance of the legend of Rudolph Valentino has not. Undaunted by time, it endures. It is timeless, just like his legend and his performances.

What draws people here, at the now renamed Hollywood Forever Cemetery year after year to pay tribute? The drama, the antics, and high hysterics? To witness the fighting factions of the different Valentino guilds who gleefully tore each other down with the hope of becoming more prominent? The legend of the Lady In Black?

Here for the first time, the history behind the Rudolph Valentino Memorial Service is revealed in detail. It is augmented by my unlimited access to previously unseen, unpublished letters, documents, and materials. Virtually every photograph in this book has never been previously published. This book will attempt to illustrate the continuing and growing phenomena that has prevailed, unabated, from his death in 1926 to this very day. Thus proving that the legacy of Rudolph Valentino has withstood the test of time.

Tracy Ryan Terhune

Table of Contents

The Valentino Memorial Cast

Here is an alphabetical list of key participants both directly and indirectly in the Valentino Memorial Services throughout it's long history. This list will advise you on what part they played in Valentino Forever - The History of the Rudolph Valentino Memorial Services.

Acker, Jean – Valentino's first wife. Their marriage lasted no longer than the reception that followed. It was so brief no photograph of the two of them together exists. She was the only wife to come to his crypt on day of the Valentino Memorial Service, in 1940.

Benda, Marion – Follies beauty who was Valentino's date on the night he fell ill in New York. Emotionally unstable, in later years she claimed to have married him and have children by him. Both claims were false. Also was photographed at the mausoleum in Lady In Black attire and she often claimed to be the original Lady In Black. After numerous suicide attempts she succeeded in ending her life in 1951.

Burnham, Roger Noble – sculptor of the *Aspiration* statue that was dedicated on May 5, 1930 and is still standing today at DeLongpre Park in Hollywood California.

Cassity, Tyler – Purchased the cemetery in 1998 and renamed it Hollywood Forever. He swiftly began to reverse the years of neglect inflicted upon the cemetery.

Del Regil, Estrellita – Eccentric woman who claimed her mother was the original Lady In Black, and became one herself, to carry on her mother's tradition. Her tenure at the crypt centered around 1976 through 1993 and she came back a few years later, wheelchair bound. Her own sister disputed any truth to her story.

Estrellita's story varied over the years. Was extremely erratic in her behavior; she never was an invited participant in any of the services.

Dexter, Anthony – Bore a significant resemblance to Valentino and was cast in the title role in the 1951 Columbia Picture *Valentino*. Showed up at the 25th anniversary to be photographed with Ditra Flame in front of the Valentino crypt.

Flame, Ditra – Legendary, and most famous of all the Ladies In Black. Had met Valentino as a 14 year old girl, and parlayed that encounter, and a few others, including a visit in the hospital into a life long commitment. Guarded her title with a fervor. She was the founder of the Valentino Memorial Guild of Hollywood.

Harris, George – Ditra Flame's yes-man who also was vice president of her Valentino Guild. Often wrote letters for Ditra, for issues she didn't want her name associated with. Also, was at Ditra's side each year she made her pilgrimage.

Kirkwood, James – A silent film star in his own right, he gave the eulogy each year for Valentino until his own death in 1963. Was also married at one time to Valentino's leading lady in *Blood and Sand*, Lila Lee.

MacLaren, Mary – Silent star, whose dressing room was next to Valentino's at Universal Studios. MacLaren holds the record for appearances as a beloved guest speaker at the Valentino Memorial Service. MacLaren spoke a record 17 consecutive years.

Martell, Belle – Represented the Troupers Club of Hollywood each year at the memorials from the mid 1950's – 1960's. Was well known for putting her finger in the air and saying "Until next year!" at the conclusion of each service.

Negri, Pola - Valentino's escort in Los Angeles. Falsely claimed to be his fiancée after his death and well known for her emotional mourning and fainting at both his funerals in New York and Los Angeles. Lost her last shred of credibility when she married just a couple of months following Valentino's death.

Peterson, Roger – Caretaker of the mausoleum where Valentino is buried, from 1929 to 1940. Authored the book *Valentino the Unforgotten* in 1937 using his day-to-day experiences at the Valentino crypt as the foundation of the book.

Philbin, Mary – Immensely popular silent star, most notably as co-star of the timeless classic *Phantom of the Opera* with Lon Chaney, Philbin was the keynote speaker at the age of 86, in 1988. She had personally known Valentino and had attended Valentino's New York and Los Angeles funeral services in 1926. Mary Philbin was the most famous silent star to appear on the roster of guest speakers in the history of the Valentino Memorial Services.

Rambova, Natacha – Second, and final wife of Valentino. Divorced the year before his death. There is no evidence that Rambova ever visited Valentino's crypt. She did, however extend an offer of a burial space in the Hudnut family plot in New York for burial in 1926.

Testa, Bud – Public relations man hired by Jack Roth to oversee the Valentino Memorial each year, after the fiasco of 1951. It was Bud Testa who first introduced the concept of a structured memorial service that is continued to the present day.

Ullman, George – Valentino's business manager who some felt took advantage of Valentino by maneuvering anyone whom he considered competition to be squeezed out of the picture. This included Natacha Rambova. Wrote a ghost-written account of his time with Valentino titled *Valentino As I Knew Him.* Ullman attended many of the Valentino Memorial Services prior to his death in 1975. A second untitled Valentino biography Ullman wrote in 1972 (soon to be published) may prove to be more forthcoming than the original.

Valentino, Alberto – Rudolph Valentino's brother who inherited one third of the estate. Is also buried at the cemetery in the Abbey of the Psalms mausoleum.

Valentino, Jean – Rudolph Valentino's nephew, son of Alberto. Jean seemed ill at ease with inheriting the Valentino legacy. Well known for his numerous lawsuits levied against Disneyland, Columbia Pictures and George Ullman.

In a moment of reverence, school children from Mott and Grand Street School in New York, willingly pose before a floral tribute picturing Rudolph Valentino against an American flag made up of flowers, before it is delivered to Campbell's Funeral Church

September 7, 1926 Church of the Good Shepherd in Beverly Hills. Top of steps:
Alberto Valentino, Pola Negri, followed by Mr. & Mrs. George Ullman

At conclusion alter boys begin the escort of the casket out of the church

Pallbearers including Charlie Chaplin carry the casket of Rudolph Valentino out of the church

Casket is carried to waiting hearse for final journey to Hollywood Memorial Park Cemetery

Funeral cars line Santa Monica Blvd. as crowds line the streets

Beverly Hills police have an easier time keeping order, than their New York counterparts

Elevated view from across the street, of invited guests departing the Church of the Good Shepherd

Funeral procession on Santa Monica Blvd. Crowds observe the impressive motorcade

Impressive view from street level of the funeral procession, with the Church of the Good
Shepherd in the rear. Beverly Hills, September 7, 1926

Solemn Requiem High Mass
will be celebrated in the
Church of the Good Shepherd
Beverly Hills
for the repose of the soul of
Rudolph Valentino
on Tuesday morning, September seventh
at ten o'clock

ADMITTANCE BY CARD

"I call for the prayers of all those
who have known me, of all those who
have loved me."
—SAINT EPHREM

IN YOUR CHARITY
Pray for the Repose of the soul of

Rodolfo Guglielmi Valentino
Died August 23, 1926

PRAYER

O Gentlest Heart of Jesus, ever
present in the Blessed Sacrament,
ever consumed with burning love for
the poor captive souls in Purgatory,
have mercy on the soul of Thy departed
servant. Be not severe in Thy judg-
ment but let some drops of Thy Pre-
cious Blood fall upon the devouring
flames, and do Thou O merciful Saviour
send Thy angels to conduct Thy departed servant to a place of refresh-
ment, light and peace. Amen.

May the souls of the faithful departed,
through the mercy of God, rest in peace.
Amen.

Funeral invitation that had to be presented in order to gain admittance to the church. Also a memorial prayer
card given to attendees as they entered the Church of the Good Shepherd

Funeral procession turning into the cemetery grounds of Hollywood Memorial Park Cemetery

Funeral procession arrives at the Cathedral Mausoleum, having just crossed the bridge that
is now adjacent to the Fairbanks grave

The last rays of sunshine fall on the casket of Rudolph Valentino, as it is unloaded from the hearse and prepares to go up the front steps of the Cathedral Mausoleum, September 7, 1926

Photographers and spectators stand across from entrance to the Cathedral Mausoleum as one of two planes hired by Luther Mahoney, that had dropped roses in front of the funeral procession, is seen flying overhead.

Leaving after the interment ceremony Pola Negri is helped up after fainting on the front steps outside the mausuleum. Paramount executive Charles Eyton is on the left, Dr. Louis Felger, right, wearing glasses

15

Standing beside a memorial wreath inscribed 'Valentino Forever' is an impressive lineup of those attending the memorial held at the Los Angeles Breakfast Club located at 3212 Riverside Drive, near Griffith Park. Back row: at left – Roy Stewart (western actor), Joe Rock, Gareth Hughes (actor), Ruth Roland (actress), then Secretary of Labor Davis, Herb Rawlinson (actor). Kneeling in front row – left: Charlie Chaplin, Emmett Flynn (director of two Valentino pre-star films: Alimony and Virtuous Sinners)

A mournful Norman Kerry leads the tribute to Valentino, with the symbolic riderless horse,
at the Los Angeles Breakfast Club

The American flag is slowly lowered to half staff at the Los Angeles Breakfast club, to conclude
the Valentino tribute. Respectfully, his friends and colleagues stand at attention

Illustrating her devotion, Ditra Flame's artistic display shows arms stretched Heaven bound towards Rudolph Valentino, whose photo is inset within the cross. Hand inked and initialed by Lady In Black Ditra Flame. This was taken from her personal Valentino scrapbook.

Blueprints for proposed Valentino tomb by architect Matlock Price Circa 1926

Various groups scrambled to make extended plans for some type of memorial service as the first anniversary of Rudolph Valentino's death approached. Since mourners were not willing to let his memory fade, plans were swiftly put in motion to protect his legacy. Amazingly, a year after his death, Valentino's star was on a huge ascent. Movie magazines elevated him to near sainthood. Valentino home shrines were successfully sold via ads in movie magazines. Poems, letters of lifelong commitment appeared in tabloids, so it wasn't a shock that approaching the very first anniversary a memorial service was announced. Sponsored by the Actor's Guild of America, the service was held on May 30th, 1927 at Hollywood Memorial Park Cemetery. The service was held in the cemetery's small chapel and was attended by 250 people. At the conclusion of the service a decorated wreath was ceremoniously placed in front of Rudy's "new" resting-place. New? When Rudolph was interred on September 7, 1926, his crypt space was in the form of a loan; June Mathis generously loaned the Valentino family the use of her crypt space, number 1099 until final arrangements could be made. However, in an unforeseen tragedy, less than a year later, she herself was stricken by a sudden heart attack while watching a play in New York on July 26, 1927, and died within minutes. This put the Valentino heirs in an awkward position. No final arrangements had yet to materialize, and plans for a colossal monument/resting place for the "Great Lover" funded by donor contributions, seemed to be unraveling. So, on August 5,1927, while June Mathis' casket was on display for visitation at the W.M. Strother funeral parlors at 6240 Hollywood Blvd., Rudolph's temporary resting place was cracked open, and his casket was transferred immediately adjacent to crypt number 1205, ultimately intended for June Mathis' surviving husband, Sylvano Balboni. At the time this was deemed a short-term solution until final plans materialized. No one on the cemetery staff that made the move of his remains on that day would ever guess that 80 years later, the body of Rudolph Valentino would still be resting there. The cost of the crypt Rudolph Valentino now occupies had been sold to June Mathis for a mere $100.00.

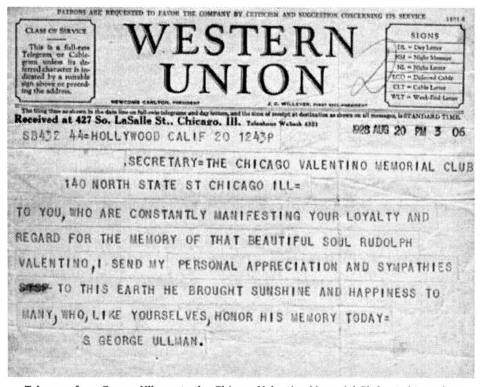

Mr. and Mrs. Alberto Guglielmi Valentino
desire the presence of
yourself and family at
Solemn Requiem High Mass
on the first anniversary of the death of
their beloved Rudolph
to be held at Blessed Sacrament Church
6657 Sunset boulevard
in Hollywood on Tuesday, August 23rd., 1927
at 10:30 a.m.

Invitation from Alberto Valentino to attend the Mass held on the first anniversary August 23, 1927

WESTERN UNION

Received at 427 So. LaSalle St.. Chicago. Ill.

SB452 44=HOLLYWOOD CALIF 20 1243P

,SECRETARY=THE CHICAGO VALENTINO MEMORIAL CLUB

140 NORTH STATE ST CHICAGO ILL=

TO YOU, WHO ARE CONSTANTLY MANIFESTING YOUR LOYALTY AND

REGARD FOR THE MEMORY OF THAT BEAUTIFUL SOUL RUDOLPH

VALENTINO,I SEND MY PERSONAL APPRECIATION AND SYMPATHIES

STOP TO THIS EARTH HE BROUGHT SUNSHINE AND HAPPINESS TO

MANY, WHO, LIKE YOURSELVES, HONOR HIS MEMORY TODAY=

S GEORGE ULLMAN.

Telegram from George Ullman to the Chicago Valentino Memorial Club – to be read at
their meeting on the second anniversary of his death.

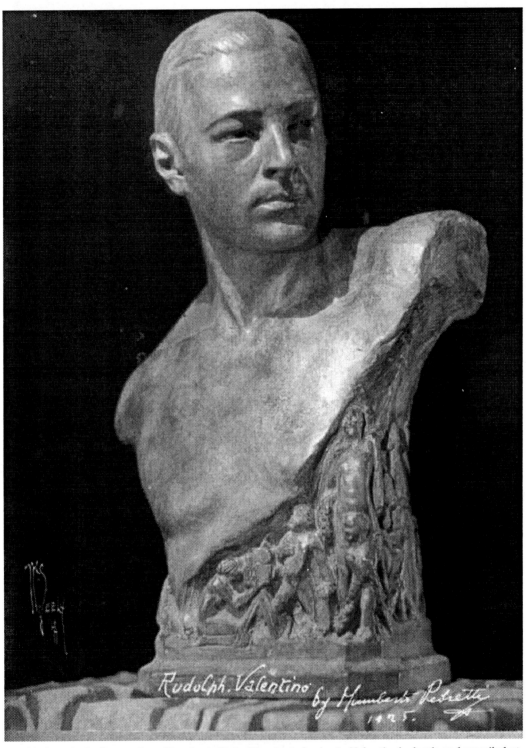

Marble bust by Italian sculptor Humberto Pedrotti – started prior to Valentino's death and unveiled at the first anniversary memorial Service on August 23, 1927

22

Alberto Valentino arranged and conducted a memorial service on behalf of the family which was held on the exact date of death, on August 23rd 1927. As in the case of the funerals held on both coasts, this, too was by invitation only. Printed cards with matching graphics and style of the original 1926 funeral invitations were mailed to those whom the Valentino family had hand selected. Announcing that "yourself and family" were invited, on the first anniversary of the death of "their beloved Rudolph" memorial services were conducted at 6657 Sunset Boulevard at the Blessed Sacrament Church. Starting time was announced as 10:30 a.m. sharp.

This family-sanctioned first anniversary commemoration succeeded in attracting a 1927's Who's Who of Hollywood elite. One newspaper gave a firsthand accounting of what went on at this family sponsored memorial, stating: "Hollywood remembered Rudolph Valentino today. More than 1,000 men and women, producers, stars, extras gathered at the Church of the Blessed Sacrament. There were present relatives and friends of the screen actor, but Pola Negri, who wept and mourned immediately after his death, did not appear. Solemn high requiem mass was chanted before a candlelit altar beneath a gold crucifix by Fathers Galli, Tonelli, and Pillolli, all Italians.

No earthly tribute we could ere bestow
Would aught repay the debt we owe,
Of gratitude, for all the joy he gave.
We leave with God our laurel wreath
    to place upon his brow;
A wreath of love, with prayers entwined,
That we may now so live that we shall
        reach at last
The Place that seems more dear ———
        Since "Rudy" passed.

Chicago Valentino Memorial Club

A tremendous wreath of tea roses and lilacs trimmed with autumn leaves and ferns from the United Artists studios was before the altar. Other wreaths and bouquets of flowers from all over the world had been sent to the mausoleum in the Hollywood cemetery where Valentino's body was placed.

Services were opened this morning by the string quartet that played for Valentino during the screening of many pictures that won him fame. They played two of Valentino's favorite selections, an aria by Bach and the Andante Cantabile by Tschaikowsky. Alberto Guglielmi, the star's brother received friends at the ceremony. The Italian government was officially represented by Count Gradenigo, vice counsel in Los Angeles. The French government was represented by the Hon Henri Didot. After the services, a statue of Valentino, crafted by Italian sculptor, Humberto Pedrotti, (completed shortly after the actors death) was unveiled for the first time before a black velvet curtain in a room especially set aside and illuminated in the church. The statue was said by his brother to be an exact likeness, right down to a small razor cut on his right cheek. Approximately sixty-five percent of those present this morning were women. But there were many key players in the motion picture industry present. Among the notables were Agnes Ayres, Monte Banks, Robert Vignola, James Quirk, M.C. Levee, producer; John W. Considine Jr., producer; Cora McGreachy, celebrated designer; Sylvano Balboni, husband of the late June Mathis; Fred Beetson, representing the Will Hays organization, Harry Barrett, secretary of the Hollywood Chamber of Commerce; and the Count and Countess Carccio. Also present was Mrs. Theresa Werner, aunt of Valentino's last wife, Natacha Rambova. No one wept during the chanting of the High Mass, but grief-stricken faces and moist eyes clearly explained that the memory of Valentino still lived in Hollywood. So did the long line of automobiles that went to the cemetery after the ceremony, as well as the fact that all the studios in Hollywood stopped work for five minutes at noon. And so, the first annual ceremonies had come to an amazing conclusion. Citing the short-term memory of the public, many wondered if there would be any continued interest beyond the first year's memorial service. It only took 12 short months to find their answer.

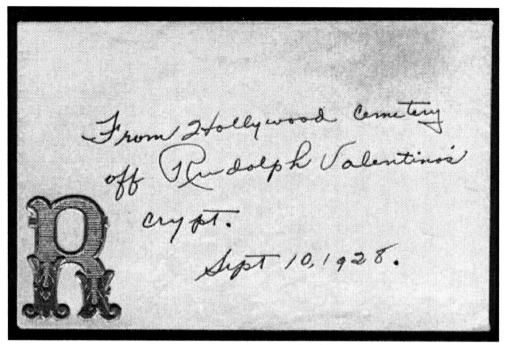

Gold foil "R" lifted as a souvenir from a ribbon spelling out Rudolph's name on a
wreath placed at his crypt. Dated September 10, 1928

Members of the Chicago Valentino Memorial Club gaze at the photo of Rudy on the
occasion of their gathering on the first anniversary of his death.

George Ullman, left, watches as artist Hubbard G. Robinson puts the finishing touches on a charcoal portrait of Rudolph Valentino commissioned for display at the Valentino Memorial Service on August 23, 1928

Candid close up of floral arraignments outside the front steps of the Cathedral Mausoleum
for the Valentino Memorial Services on August 23,1929

As the second annual service drew near, the plans were unfolded. In 1928 George Ullman had commissioned artist Hubbard G. Robinson to create a pastel five-foot portrait to adorn the ceremonies. This year the majority of the floral arrangements were placed outside the mausoleum, adjacent to the entrance steps. This staggering display included an almost twenty foot cross with the inscription that read "We Never Forget." Although attendance was estimated at 3,000 people, the ceremonies were noted by reporters for their simplicity. Speakers included Father Joseph A. Sullivan President of Loyola College, who spoke of Valentino's legacy in history. On behalf of the family, Alberto Valentino also was on hand and took center stage to humbly thank the huge throng for remembering Rudolph. Attending for the first time was his son, Jean Valentino. Even Rudolph's young nephew was deemed newsworthy. On July 8, 1928 it was announced in the papers that "Jean Valentino, 14 year old nephew of the late Rudolph Valentino, arrived today on the liner Vulcania, traveling to Hollywood on a pilgrimage to the tomb of his uncle. The boy bears a slight resemblance to the dead actor, but says he has no stage or screen ambitions. He is studying to become an electrical engineer." Afterwards, the three-piece orchestra that had accompanied Rudy on his Mineralava tour were reassembled to play a few solemn selections. Simultaneously, in London, scores of men and women, most garbed in black, paid tribute by gathering at the roof top garden of the Italian Hospital at Queens Square. Many of the English women were adorned with red roses, Valentino's favorite flower. A fence bordering the Valentino garden had a life-size photograph of Rudy wreathed in laurels. In Chicago, at the Chicago's Playhouse Theater, located at 410 South Michigan Boulevard, memorial ceremonies were conducted with guest speakers including the Reverend R. Keene Ryan who repeatedly referred to Valentino as "that brilliant boy" and "that talented boy," and was duly interrupted several times by spontaneous bursts of applause. He went on to beseech the American government to lift all immigration restrictions so that America would benefit by getting more artists such as Rudolph Valentino. Noted photographer Mabel Sykes (secretary of the Chicago Valentino Club) read a couple of telegrams; Screen star Bebe Daniels, wired "God Bless Rudy, his memory will live with us always. It will afford me a great deal of happiness to be enrolled as a member of the Chicago Valentino Memorial Club. My best wishes." Mabel then read a telegram from S. George Ullman who cabled "To you, who are constantly manifesting your loyalty and regard for the memory of that beautiful soul, Rudolph Valentino, I send my personal appreciation and sympathies. To this earth he brought sunshine and happiness to many, who, like yourselves, honor his memory today." She noted that the club was inspired entirely by sentiment and that it had no financial connection with the movie industry. To wrap up the festivities, a print of Monsieur Beaucaire was shown. Ditra Flame's Valentino Memorial Guild ran memorial ads in movie magazines that stated "To Our Beloved Rudy, from the Valentino Memorial Guild in America, Europe, India, South Africa, Canada and Australia, and used as their slogan the quote "The battle goes well, beloved, and your flag still flies."

Alberto Valentino, center, greets unidentified fan at the foot of the front steps of the mausuleum. His son, Jean Valentino, left, is partly hidden by the large rose bloom. Circa 1928

The events around the globe in 1928 proved that without a shadow of a doubt that the Valentino legacy was intact and if anything, skyrocketing.

The year 1929 was a turning point in motion pictures. "Talkies" were rapidly replacing silent pictures. Sound was the new king. Foreign stars with heavy accents found that their careers were ruined by the existence of the microphone and suddenly "retired." But the Valentino faithful were ever vigilant, with an eye to the past yet a hope for the future, and on August 23rd showed up in force to mark the third anniversary of his passing. Once more, Rudy's brother Alberto brought his son to witness the ceremonies. Again, the floral array was predominately placed outside the mausoleum and the display was quite impressive. A sphere in the same shape and form of the Washington Monument was predominant and surrounded by a wealth of industry-sent bouquets and wreathes.

A photograph of Ditra Flame and two friends in front of this floral display exists, to show us that she was indeed there and thus validating her claim to the title of Lady In Black. However, the photo depicts Ditra in typical 1920's flapper style attire, certainly, no veil or anything of what would soon become the typical trademark style of dress associated with the Lady In Black. But she nevertheless set the stage for what was to come in the next eight decades. Again, to the delight of many, the trio of musicians appeared to play songs that were labeled as Rudy's favorite melodies. Valentino's former manger George Ullman oversaw the details of the service. He made note that within "the next two or three weeks," an announcement would be forthcoming in regards to inquiries made by concerned fans, as to the permanent resting place properly befitting their beloved Rudy. He said the grandiose plans would be solely funded by the many various Valentino associations around the world. No one doubted he knew of what he spoke and most nodded with unabated agreement.

Earliest known photo of Lady In Black Ditra Flame (far left) attending the Valentino Memorial Service
Circa August 23, 1929

If there was any doubt, 1929 showed the depth of emotion felt by the Valentino faithful. But the following year proved to be a turning point, the start of a new decade and with the October 1929 stock market crash, the start of the depression. More than ever, people would seek escape in the movies. And those who looked back on the roaring 1920's as their youth, and carefree 'good old days' would join the crusade already in progress and make 1930 a remarkable year.

Fourth annual Valentino Memorial Service - August 23, 1930. Flappers line the walls within the alcove of Valentino's resting place on that solemn day.

1930-1939

The Valentino Memorial Committee had been working valiantly for the previous four years to accomplish something that had never been done before. As a way of remembering and honoring Valentino, they achieved a landmark ruling. The committee had obtained permission to erect the first statue ever dedicated in honor of a motion picture star. Their goal to raise enough funds for the statue was realized in three short years. The chosen location was a quaint rural neighborhood in Hollywood, featuring a small square shaped park. It was named DeLongpre Park in honor of well-known early California artist, Paul DeLongpre who was famous for his paintings of flowers. After much negotiation with city officials the approval was given, and a work was commissioned from sculptor Roger Noble Burnham. To appease the nay sayers it was agreed that Burnham would not make the monument an exact likeness, but rather an artistic expression of Valentino's place of esteem in the Hollywood community. So, on May 6th 1930, on what would have been Rudolph Valentino's thirty-fifth birthday, the dedication ceremonies commenced. It was announced that it had been paid for "by the humble and sincere offerings of nickels and dimes from thousands of his fans." Chiseled just below the four foot bronze statue, plated in gleaming gold, with the figure's head turned skyward, and below the marble ball representing the global world of Valentino's fans, it was inscribed "Erected in memory of Rudolph Valentino 1895-1926 Presented by his friends and admirers from every walk of life in all parts of the world. In appreciation of the happiness brought to them by his cinema portrayals." At the top of the dedication was the statue's title, *Aspiration.* Almost 1,500 persons packed the ceremony, although few Hollywood notables were present, Rudolph's fans from every walk of life were there in abundance. Delores Del Rio was assisted by sculptor Roger Burnham in unveiling this historic statue. George Ullman was present and was clearly heard to tear up and say "I'm glad for you, Rudy. You will never be forgotten." Amazingly, the someone who was forgotten, was Alberto Valentino; no one thought to invite him or his family to the event. Interviewed two years later by Jack Grant, Alberto first publicly spoke of his slight at the dedication. When Mr. Grant said "You must have been deeply touched at the unveiling," Alberto quietly mentioned that "I did not attend the unveiling." When questioned as to why, Alberto, not wishing to offend by this date, simply stated "I was not invited. Perhaps it was an oversight." But the significance of the statue was not lost on Alberto who went on to recognize that "They did a beautiful thing in giving him a statue. I am proud in the knowledge that it is the first time such an honor has been paid a motion picture star."

Original photo of the miniature model of Aspiration, as submitted for city consent.
It was given the final seal of approval on March 5, 1930, only two
short months before it was unveiled on May 5, 1930

With the miniature model seen to the left, Roger Noble Burnham proudly poses in his studio with the full size *Aspiration* statue, shortly before it is permanently moved to DeLongpre Park

1930's Valentino admirer poses next to the Aspiration statue. Unique in it's being the only statue in Hollywood ever erected to a single motion picture star. Amazingly, that record still stands today.

By the time August 23rd 1930 came around the memorial was held with a little over 200 people in attendance. Newspapers were quick to note this, stating that that on the day he died the public mourners were massive in numbers. They went on to point out that "there were practically no picture people at the memorial service." Again the three-piece orchestra played, and Alec Francis spoke words of sympathy. George Ullman and Alberto were spotted in attendance and during the service both were witnessed to have shed tears. Visibly sobbing was Cora MacGeachy. She had been a personal friend of Valentino's since 1923 and had come to California in 1925 on Valentino's bequest as a seamstress for his film *The Eagle*. She was very deeply involved with spiritual messages and hosted several séances in New York with Rudy and his wife Natacha. Rudy had gifted Cora with an oversized photo of himself on the starboard of his yacht, dressed in a tank top and white trousers, with his hands on his hips. For the rest of her life she kept this in the original silver frame in which Valentino had presented it to her in.

People concluded the service by mulling around and reading the inscription cards on the floral arrangements.

With the advent of the Depression, the public focus was primarily diverted to economic issues. However as the 1930's rolled on, it seemed nothing could deter the Valentino faithful from their annual pilgrimage. On the fifth anniversary it was reported that "a steady stream visited the Hollywood mausoleum where his body lies and also carried wreaths of flowers to his memorial statue, Aspiration in DeLongpre Park." A Lady In Black had started to appear and be noticed, but she did not step forward to identify herself or give an explanation as to her actions. Early reports cited her as "a mysterious blonde woman in black." Perhaps Ditra also attended. If so, she melded in with the crush of other mourners who visited his grave by the hundreds. The same year, the London Guild was just as busy acknowledging the fifth anniversary. Their itinerary listed their events stating that "Today is to be entirely devoted to his memory by members of the Valentino Association." They went on to detail the day's lineup. It included a 10:30 a.m.

High Mass at Westminster Cathedral, 4:15 p.m. tea for members of the association and 50 cadets of the Dulwich Navel Brigade. 4:45 p.m. tea to the patients and staff of the Italian Hospital, Queens Square. 5:15 p.m. a march pass by the navel cadets in the courtyard of the Forum Cinema Villers-Street, W. C. 5:30 p.m. in the Forum Cinema, a special program of music associated with Valentino's films, followed by the screening of *Blood and Sand.* After the film, it was announced that the record Valentino had recorded for Brunswick in 1923 would be played. For most, this would be the first opportunity to hear his voice. Lest people say the London Guild was indulging in hero worship, Miss Elliot, who was honorary secretary to the Guild stated for the sake of the press that "We are not a hysterical society. In spite of what people say, our purpose is definitely practical, largely devoted to children. Already 35 children from the poorest parts of London have been given a fortnight by the sea, as our guests, while 400 have passed through the Valentino Ward at the Italian Hospital."

Overhead view of Hollywood Memorial Cemetery Circa 1930
Proving Rudolph Valentino is not forgotten. Below, Rita Flynn poses
next to a wreath placed at his crypt on August 23, 1931

The year 1932 was most revealing to Valentino followers. Cemetery caretaker of the Cathedral Mausoleum for the past three years, Roger C. Peterson had kept an extensive diary of the daily comings and goings of the innumerable people who sought out Valentino's resting-place. In April 1932 he wrote his first article based on those transcripts. Published in the monthly magazine called *The New Movie Magazine*, it was titled *My Strange Experiences at Valentino's Grave*, featuring an eyewitness account. His first-hand experiences make great reading. Peterson was, by his own admission, a straightforward, no nonsense type of man. He had little empathy for the hordes of souvenir hunters and the almost daily over the top hysterical women he encountered. Even at this early stage, he attempted to understand the reason behind the level of devotion people felt towards Valentino. Peterson said that "Nine out of every ten visitors to the mausoleum stop at Valentino's crypt. Those who are familiar with it's location find their way to the spot unattended. Many of these come back repeatedly. Some appear regularly on the same day of the month or week and at the same hour. Most are solemn and reverent. Some give way to tears each time. Many come once and are never seen again. There must be a reason for these things. I cannot believe that things just happen. There is something deeper and more vital in this interest in Rudolph Valentino, than the mere memory of his short and brilliant career. Thousands who are drawn to his tomb are moved by more than the memory of his shadow on the screens of the world. If not, why is he singled out for adulation-almost worship-while greater actors and greater men are forgotten? Why is his resting-place visited every day of the year by this continuous procession of men and women from near and far? Why do they stand with moist eyes and bowed heads before his crypt? Why do they break into sobs? Why do they kneel in prayer? Why do I receive letters from every corner of the earth from people who want descriptions of the tomb? Why the constant floral offerings? There must be something deeper than idle curiosity or mere hero worship." Obviously Peterson had more questions than answers. But what he witnessed was unique. His interaction with these visitors gave valuable insight into how people felt about Rudy. He stated in one case that "A woman about forty-five years old came to the mausoleum. She asked the attendant, who was taking my place, the whereabouts of Rudy's crypt. She requested that she be left alone there, as she wished to communicate with Rudy's spirit if possible. She went on to say that she was a medium and had talked with Rudy many times in her own home, but that he had always disappeared before she had the opportunity to ask him as many questions as she wished. She therefore had come to the cemetery that she might better converse with him. The attendant left and a short time later the lady came running to him, and cried, "Come quick, Rudy knocks! Rudy knocks!" She grabbed him by the arm, all excited, and together they ran to Rudy's crypt. Sure enough, a tapping could be heard from above. By this time other people who were in the mausoleum came to find out what the excitement was. The attendant quietly left the group and, with an assistant, crawled up into the attic. Making their way to the place where the tappings were, they found a large bird caught in the air vent. They soon freed it and went back to tell the people at the crypt the cause of the tappings. The face of the medium turned all colors." Peterson shrugged off the incident with amusement. However another visitor made him realize something very unique was happening. Again he had more questions than answers. He told of how "She walked into the mausoleum with the grace of a deer. She carried a small rabbit, cuddled in her arms. Approaching me she asked, "Is there some water that I may give my bunny a drink? We have come a long way and I know he must be thirsty." I brought water and both refreshed themselves. Then, to my surprise, she said, "You must be the man I dreamed about, over a month ago. Yes, you are the image of him. I had a horrible dream. I was walking along a high cliff, I had a the feeling that I must get down somehow. There were steps, but the height made me dizzy. Then came that dreadful feeling one has at times when looking down from a great height, the urge to jump came to me. As I was about to leap into space, out of the shadows came Rudolph Valentino riding a great white horse. He spoke to me, and how his words cling in my memory. He said, 'Do not destroy that which is beautiful. God has given you life for you to live. Fear not the future. Your life has been a lesson, carry on and profit by your experiences. The greatest goal is true love. Look and you shall see. Fear not to go down those steps. A man who watches my place of rest will meet you and see that you will be safe.' With those words he was gone. I awoke and remembered the words of Valentino about the man who guarded his resting-place, so I decided to go and see if dreams really have a meaning, and here I am. This is the greatest adventure I have ever undertaken, trying to solve a dream, and succeeding. Please show me Valentino's tomb." Still astonished at the whole thing, I led her to the crypt. Did the spirit of Valentino guide her to me? She has repeatedly said that the description of the man in the dream was I, in size appearance and dress."

Custodian of the mausoleum Roger C. Peterson, right, poses on the front steps with Valentino fan Leon Massey.
Circa August 1938

Roger Peterson may have had many questions of his own, but the prevailing puzzle was the identity of the mysterious woman who was seen arriving at Valentino's crypt every August 23rd starting in 1930 at the dedication of the Valentino *Aspiration* memorial statue. Reportedly the creation of publicity man Russell Birdwell for a short film entitled *The Only Normal Man in Hollywood*, Birdwell claimed that he had paid an unnamed actress a mere $5.00 to pose as a mourner at the Valentino statue. He speculated that perhaps she enjoyed the mystique and notoriety so much that she continued on her own, expanding her 'role,' appearing at Valentino's crypt in the following years. When the Lady In Black as the press named her, began showing up at Valentino's crypt heavily veiled and all in black, she steadfastly refused to identify herself as she placed her floral tribute and paused in prayer. Leaving as quickly as she arrived, she departed, keeping everyone guessing as to her identity. Some whispered that it must be Pola Negri, fulfilling her promise to keep their flame of love alive. Over the top, Pola, who had cried out that "The world does not know my grief" on the steps of the mausoleum the day Valentino was buried, married a quick eight months later, never to return to the site. Others guessed that perhaps it was Jean Acker, who had been in New York at the time of death and had been seen together with Rudy in his last remaining days, since apparently they smoothed over their very public divorce. But the truth of the matter was no one actually knew who the mysterious Lady In Black was. Simply put - she wasn't talking. Thus, a legend was born.

On March 24, 1933 the Valentino estate filed papers seeking the court's hurried acceptance of the purchase of crypt number 1205 from Sylvano Balboni. As Balboni was returning to his native Italy, the court agreed to the expedited process and a payment of $800.00 was issued to him. This purchase was never publicly announced, yet from this day forward, Rudolph Valentino no longer rested in a borrowed crypt.

PATRONS ARE REQUESTED TO FAVOR THE COMPANY BY CRITICISM AND SUGGESTION CONCERNING ITS SERVICE

1264

CLASS OF SERVICE

This is a full-rate Telegram or Cablegram unless its deferred character is indicated by a suitable sign above or preceding the address.

WESTERN UNION

SIGNS

DL = Day Letter

NM = Night Message

NL = Night Letter

LCO = Deferred Cable

NLT = Cable Night Letter

WLT = Week-End Letter

NEWCOMB CARLTON, PRESIDENT   J. C. WILLEVER, FIRST VICE-PRESIDENT

The filing time as shown in the date line on full-rate telegrams and day letters, and the time of receipt at destination as shown on all messages, is STANDARD TIME.

Received at

3np f 43

as New York 158p Dec 7 1932

Walter Winchell

Mirror

Dear Mr Winchell Read your column this morning and take this

means of informing you that Rudys body is not going to rest in

a borrowed crypt very much longer stop I am personally making

arrangements for a permanent resting place very sincerely

Pola Negri.

Telegram sent to noted columnist Walter Winchell, from Pola Negri saying she was personally taking charge of the issue of final arrangements for Valentino. In reality, Pola was never involved in the purchase of Valentino's burial place.

On July 12, 1933 Alberto wrote a letter to the Chicago Memorial Guild informing them that "I am very grateful to you and to all the members of the Chicago Valentino Memorial Club, to whom I wish to convey through you, my sincerest greetings, for the constant and beautiful thought of keeping our beloved Rudy's memory sacred, and alive." Feeling the pinch in the depths of the depression, Alberto went on to confide that "Last year I was unable to arrange, as usual, the family memorial service in Hollywood, for lack of financial means. I hope this year to have better luck." Although Alberto discontinued the family's private memorials, the trek to Valentino's crypt only increased each year. Roger Peterson continued to document these visits. He witnessed when "A beautiful girl used to come here every Sunday. She would not say a word of who she was. She always brought a potted plant and watered it with her tears, for it seemed she was continually crying. One day I asked her if I could be of any help. She replied, 'Yes. Please take care of the plant that I have here, for I am going away and I may never return.' Her blue eyes filled again with tears. I said I would do as she wished, and told her I was sorry to see her cry so much. 'Rudy meant so much to me,' she murmured. 'I loved him because—because'— her voice faltered. Again she looked at me. 'Because he loved me.' With those words she fell to weeping again. I left her alone. When I returned she was gone. I never saw her again. I will never forget the lonesome look she had." Floral arrangements arrived daily from all parts of the world. Some sent Peterson money to purchase these on their behalf, and others were wired and delivered by local florists. Peterson noted that "Soon after Valentino died, two large beaded memorial wreaths were delivered at the mausoleum. One of them was from his good friend Clarence Victor Miller, who had it made in France and brought it over to this country when he came back from abroad. Who gave the other wreath I do not know. I think it was made in Italy and sent by some admirer. These wreaths are composed of thousands of small beads, which are strung on fine wire and woven into flower designs of various colors and patterns. They were placed at Valentino's crypt and remained there until 1930. I then removed them because they were getting shabby from being mutilated by souvenir hunters. Whenever people express a wish for some

46

token of remembrance of Rudy, I give them a few beads from the wreaths. These little souvenirs are now scattered all over the world. One afternoon two swarthy turbaned Hindus came into the mausoleum. They inquired about the resting-place of a missionary whom they had known in India. I looked for the name they gave, in my book where I keep all my records. I pointed out the crypt and they stood before it and talked to one another in their native tongue. They finally spoke to me and asked if they could see the resting-place of Valentino. I showed them his crypt. They stood before it and, it seemed to me, repeated the same conversation. They asked me a lot of questions about Valentino. One, whom I judged to be the older, said, 'Mr. Valentino was a genius. He created a change in motion pictures that brought romance to the world and happiness to thousands. May his spirit rest in peace.'"

Memorial Day was May 30,1934; newspapers the following day stated with bold type that a "mysterious beauty again pays Valentino tribute." Already the legend was taking hold, the newspapers further reporting that "annually a mysterious and beautifully gowned woman visits the borrowed crypt in which lies the body of the great film sheik in a Hollywood cemetery. It was learned today that the woman made her yearly visit and deposited a wreath of purple colored flowers on the crypt of the man who had many loves. Then she vanished, leaving cemetery attaches as puzzled over her identity as they were when she made her initial visit on the first Memorial Day after Valentino died. The flowers were purchased as in the past from a small shop near the cemetery. The florist told friends that the woman, as usual, was heavily veiled. 'But she was beautiful, the veil could not conceal that. She had the manner of a queen. She spoke slowly. I could detect more tragedy in her voice even than was there when I first saw her. She came in a large limousine,' the florist was quoted."

In the initial years after his death, memorials were being held at various times. As in the very first memorial service for Valentino, many used the Memorial Day holiday to set aside as the day to remember. Some chose the date of his birth, to celebrate the gift his life gave to the world. And then still some would begin to chose the actual date of his leaving this world, August 23rd. Within a short few years the August date became predominant and the other dates fell by the wayside as far as additional memorial services were concerned. The tradition was taking hold.

On August 19, 1934, just a few days prior to the 1934 memorial, Alberto Valentino wrote to Adeline Linnell, (the treasurer of the Chicago Memorial Club) and said that "I want to repeat to you all my appreciation for the beautiful work the Valentino Memorial Club is doing for keeping Rudy's memory always alive and sacred and, in the meantime, express my grateful thanks for the kind invitation at the memorial service on the anniversary of His departure." He closed the letter stating "I hope to be in Chicago in the near future and have the pleasure of conveying personally to you and all the members of the Valentino Club the expression of Rudy's family gratitude." Interesting to note is that as early as 1928 an article appeared with the title *Are they Making Valentino A Saint?* One didn't have to look too long or too far to find the evidence. In the Chicago Valentino Memorial Guild's charter, every reference to Valentino, in the pronoun was capitalized. The charter read that "through His cinema portrayals gave to the world great happiness." And that the guild is here to "honor His memory in every possible way." And to "defend His name against unjust criticism." Even in Alberto's letter to the guild he did the same by saying "on the anniversary of His departure." Only in the Holy Bible when referring to Jesus had this ever been seen in print before. Newspapers and movie magazines and even more so, people who actually knew Rudy were amazed at this dramatic shift in public reverence. Several had theories but none had any logical explanation, and shook their heads when pressed to explain this.

Once August 23rd arrived the press was in force. "Memory of Actor Valentino Honored" hailed the headlines. Reporting that "from far places came floral offerings to be laid upon the floor of the crypt and these offerings completely hid the flower pieces which local relatives and friends of the screen star had placed in his honor. Cemetery records listed floral tributes from admirers in Austria, Chicago, New York, England and Rome. Many of these came from Valentino

Memorial Clubs." As usual, "Alberto Valentino and wife Ada, paid their anniversary visit to the tomb. They have never missed a year since Alberto brought the body of his brother from New York, where he died, and arranged the funeral which is still recalled in Hollywood for its great profusion of flower tributes." Citing how Alberto got there early, the reporter noted that "there was no crowd at the crypt when the brother and sister in law stood for a few moments with bowed heads in memory and then, placing their wreaths, departed."

In 1935 the British branch of the Valentino Memorial Guild was drawing notices that "nine years after his death, the memory of Rudolph Valentino, the movie actor, is kept alive in England. The agony columns of the morning papers contained in memoriams yesterday such as the following: 'Valentino, we shall not look upon his like again. Signed, Admirer.' High Mass will be celebrated Sunday in the Westminster Cathedral for the great lover of the silent screen." The Queen Mother was an avid Valentino fan and had shown his films at Buckingham palace to an invited audience. At her passing in 2002 at the age of 101 a copy of her invitation to view *The Sheik* at the palace was reprinted in British papers. The tribute at Westminster Cathedral was a rare gesture in England for an American film star. It is not recorded whether the Queen mother was able to attend.

Placing a floral arrangement at the Valentino crypt, Roger Peterson,
right, is assisted by an unidentified man. Circa 1938

Roger Peterson continued to document the daily occurrences at Valentino's grave. After receiving an avalanche of letters from every corner of the globe, following his original article in 1932, he decided the time was right to expand his diary of visitors to Valentino's crypt into a full fledged book. Shopping his idea around, he enlisted the help of the Chicago Valentino Memorial Guild and wrote to them on March 22,1935, stating "I have about completed the book of which I told you. It occurs to me that it might be well to include in it some account of the Valentino Memorial, of which you had charge during the Fair. The interest shown, the approximate number of visitors, any striking incidents in connection with it. I shall appreciate anything you can tell me about it." He went on to press for help in his search for a publisher to have them offer an estimate as to the market for such a book he was wishing to publish. He asked of them "Will you please give me, in a form which I may present to an interested publisher, the probable sale of the book to your club membership, or to any other groups you know about." All that he observed, starting in 1929, would be vividly recalled in his book. He told of when "This young girl came seeking Valentino's tomb. She was just a little thing. In her arms was a dear baby wrapped in a blanket. I asked if I could carry it and she said I could. It was a girl. What a wonderful bunch of happiness you have here I told her. 'Happiness, you say?' She asked. I answered, Yes, a baby like this would bring happiness to anyone. As I looked into her eyes, I could see tears forming. We had reached Valentino's crypt and I did not say any more about the baby. I told her about Rudy, and she asked me many questions concerning the people who came here. Does anyone, she wanted to know, ever have any dreams about him? I replied, Yes lots of them do. The reason I asked, she went on, is because I have dreams about him so often. Then she told a story which I will give as I recall. 'I am seventeen years old and I have had a hard journey in this life so far. I wonder if it is really worth while after all. There is a man,' she pointed at Rudy's crypt, 'who was at the peak of his career, and death took everything away. As young as I am, I loved him dearly, although I only saw him in pictures. I was born in a sod shanty in Dakota. There the golden wheat grows, the air is fresh and people seem more human. I would give anything if I could go back. I can't go now, not with the baby. You see I am not married. I am one of the girls who came to Hollywood to seek work in the movies. Like many of the others, I fell because I was innocent. Why I am telling you this I do not know. Maybe it's because we are in the presence of Valentino. The baby is like a message from God, making me brave to carry on, for she is everything I have left to live for. Were it not for her I would give up trying.' I gave the baby a tug with my finger as I talked with the little mother. There is much to live for, I told her. This baby was put on this earth for a purpose, as you and I were. God only knows what that purpose is. We must live our lives the best we can and profit by our experiences. God is just, and even if the baby wasn't born as you would wish, it is the same as anyone else. My girl, that baby to you is a gift from heaven. It will change your life and teach you to think for yourself." Later as she prepared to leave Peterson stopped her and inquired as to what she meant by an earlier remark. He said "Before you go, may I ask why you wanted to know whether other people ever had dreams about Valentino? She looked at me with a wistful smile and answered, 'When I was despondent I was going to kill myself and my baby. For three nights I would have a dream about Valentino. He would tell me not to do it. So I just had to think there was something big in those dreams. That is how I came to where he is interred. So you see I have a lot to be grateful for now. I again wish to thank you for what you have done.' She shook my hand. It was a farewell I will never forget."

In 1936 the tencennial of Valentino's death was well remembered. The growing faithful, as always, were present at the services. In anticipation of this anniversary, it was reported in the newspapers that at crypt number 1205 "the white marble wall will be bright with banked baskets and wreaths." They acknowledged that "ten years have dimmed a fickle public's memory, but the sleek haired screen idol of millions is not a forgotten name."

Two days later, on August 25, 1936, Alberto Valentino, who's handwriting was quite similar to his more famous brother's, hand wrote a note to Adeline Linnell, who was the treasurer of the Chicago Valentino Memorial Club. In the short note he asked that she "Please accept the sincerest and deepest appreciation of the whole family for the floral tribute to the memory of our beloved Rudy on the tenth anniversary of his passing beyond."

Letter from Alberto Valentino marking the 10th anniversary of his brother's death

While putting the finishing touches on his book, Roger Peterson wisely kept his eyes and ears open. At the tenth anniversary services he was quoted as an authority. He stated, "There have been more visitors to see the Valentino Crypt this year than for a long time." He even acknowledged that some people who lived in far distant lands who had a slim, if any chance of ever attending a memorial service had sent him money. They asked him to purchase on their behalf, flower arrangements to be placed in the dual vases that adorned either side of his nameplate. The month before the tenth anniversary memorial service Peterson began to release installments of his book, turning it into a series of articles on what he witnessed at the Valentino crypt. From the letters pouring in, it seemed that the public couldn't get enough.

Peterson never knew from day to day what he would happen upon. One more incident he recalled in his book was "The day when many of the passengers and crew from the great ship Empress of Britain, paid homage to Valentino. The party drove up in large busses and private cars. When they unloaded and came into the mausoleum, one would have thought that a great funeral was about to take place. Officers of the ship acted as guides and spokesmen. I knew, before they asked, who it was they sought. I said, 'come this way,' and led them to Valentino's tomb.

Many foreign people were in the crowd. Many spoke in their native tongue or in broken English. Some knelt and said a prayer. Others asked if it was all right for them to place their hands on the crypt. I told them it was, and suggested that they should stand in line, so that each one could pay homage in his own way. Some such arrangement as this was necessary, with a crowd of two hundred people, because the crypt is situated at the end of a rather narrow corridor. It was an impressive sight, this orderly, reverent procession, a sight to make one marvel at the strange influence which Valentino held and still holds over thousands. Many wiped away tears as they stood before his crypt."

The year 1937 brought more people than ever to pay their respects. Papers reported that "by 8:00 a.m. women going to work had come in numbers large enough to fill a corner of the crypt. Again at noon the number grew until many had to wait until people ahead of them got out of the way." However what was becoming clear was that the focus was shifting. People were not flocking to the site just to remember the screen's greatest lover. They were also coming with hopes of catching a glimpse of the so-called mysterious lady, or the Lady In Black. They wanted to see her, to watch her make her pilgrimage, with hopes that just this time, she might reveal her true identity. The newspapers were quick to catch onto this, and they reported that year that "much interest centers around the expected arrival of a woman in black who mysteriously arrives each year on this date. She is unidentified, but always brings flowers and says a prayer, on bended knees, before the crypt." Of course not everyone who arrived that day was shrouded in black, nor attempted to remain a mystery. Miss Agnes O'Laughlin was photographed by the Los Angeles Examiner while on her knees before the tomb, her hands clasped in a prayerful pose. She came with her mother, Mrs. Maude O'Laughlin. But Agnes was different than the typical mourner. She had prior credibility to back up her story. As a young girl she had gone to the Polyclinic Hospital in New York during those dark days of August 1926, while Valentino lay ill and had brought a small token of flowers to cheer her screen idol. The fact that Valentino never got to see her token of respect did not deter her from making her first visit to his grave, eleven years later, while on a visit in Los Angeles for a family reunion. Also observed were Alberto Valentino and his wife, who placed flowers on behalf of the family. Any new angle is always looked upon with favor by the press, and this year they found it. A second Lady In Black appeared. They noted that "a new Lady In Black, lovely and mysterious as the woman who has mourned the dead star for years, made her appearance yesterday in the Rudolph Valentino legend. While eager watchers waited for the girl whose devotion to the memory of the young Italian has become Hollywood history, a second woman appeared at the crypt." They went on to notice that "she, too, wore unrelieved black, was veiled and silent as the first one who had mourned," and that "she too knelt in silent prayer before the flower banked plaque." The idea of pitting Ladies In Black against each other was too good to pass up. The press didn't know who they were, or what their real reasons were, sincere or otherwise, but they need not have worried, they didn't have long to wait.

Mr. & Mrs. Alberto Valentino pay respects at the Valentino Memorial
August 23, 1938

Miss Agnes O'Laughlin kneels before the crypt. As a young girl, she had taken flowers
to the Polyclinic Hospital when Rudy was ill.

In the May 1937 issue of movie magazine *Screen Guide* a headline appeared stating that *Valentino Sobs Believed Bunk!* They went on to declare that "on the anniversary of Rudolph Valentino's death great to do is made over placing of wreaths on his grave. Undoubtedly some of the remembrances are sincere. But, on the eleventh year of his passing, *Screen Guide* learns that one florist racketeers on Valentino grief. He sends a mourner a wreath, mails letters to Valentino fans, takes their orders for flowers for the star's grave."

The year 1937 also was a breakthrough for mausoleum caretaker Roger C. Peterson. He secured a publisher for his daily diary, which he managed to forge into a full-fledged book, entitled *Valentino - The Unforgotten*. Peterson flushed out his book with a lot of interesting extras. He included chapters on handwriting analysis of Rudolph Valentino conducted by A. Henry Silver, a well-known graphologist. A chapter was assisted by Dr. Juno Kayy Walton who did a numerology on Valentino that Peterson called "numberscope." He rounded it out with help from Paul Foster Case who gave "an astrological analysis of a man born in Castellaneta, Italy, at 3:00 a.m. on May 6, 1895. He was given the latitude and longitude, but the name of Rudolph Valentino was not mentioned." To conclude his book, Roger Peterson added letters and poems of avid fans who had corresponded with him. To those who were lucky enough to obtain a copy of this book, it revealed to them first hand, day in and day out eyewitness accounts at Valentino's grave, and that's what made this book so unique. One of Peterson's best heart-felt remembrances was that of a disfigured dwarf. He noted that "I felt sorry for him, making his way up the steps to the mausoleum. He paused as he reached the doorway." Peterson showed him, by request, to Valentino's grave, and was touched when he saw that "When the hunchback saw Valentino's name on the bronze plate he knelt on his bony knees and said a prayer. A lump rose in my throat and my heart went out to this misshapen youth as he crouched there on the marble floor. When he arose, tears were streaming down his cheeks. His voice choked as he said, 'I am not like other people. I used to picture myself as Valentino. He meant everything to me. It's kinda tough to be like me, but there

probably was some reason for it. I believe there is a great beyond where we go
when we finish this life, and I hope to get a break there.'

He asked if I minded if he stayed a while. Of course I told him that I didn't and
went and got a chair for him. Nearly three hours later, when I returned I found
the poor chap curled up in the chair, fast asleep." Upon Peterson's return he
awoke and "He asked me if he might have a flower from the bouquet on the crypt.
I told him that he could pick it out himself. That pleased him greatly. I also gave
him a few beads from the wreath. His eyes misted again as he thanked me. 'No
one has ever treated me so kindly before. Why are you so good to me?' I answered
him 'Just because you are an unfortunate is no reason for people around you to
be unkind. Whenever you are around, stop in here if you care too.' I never saw
him again. Poor soul, I hope he is all right, and that he gets his break when he
finishes this cycle of life."

The year 1938 added even more fuel to the Valentino legend. And it brought
forth yet more interesting facts. In reporting of the annual memorial service in
August, the papers were quick to note that "the memory of Rudolph Valentino
drew scores of women to his tomb today on the twelfth anniversary of his death.
Adding one more fantastic touch was the expected annual appearance of the Lady
In Black. Deeply veiled, she comes each August 23 with a spray of red roses,
places it in a wall holder and slips away." Another paper noted that this years
mystery women was different. They said that she "appeared younger, smaller and
somewhat unfamiliar with the scene. Instead of removing whatever flowers were
in the vases at the crypt and replacing them with hers, as the 'mystery woman'
has done before, she laid her bouquet on the windowsill and hurried away." Roger
Peterson was delighted to give an account of what he knew. He stated that "This
is a great day for the memory of Valentino. Every year, except last, this
mysterious veiled woman has come to pay tribute at the tomb. She is a real
woman, but I am pledged not to reveal her name, nor even to hint at her story."

Earlier in the year, in an unkind twist of fate, Roger Peterson received bad
news from his publisher, the Wetzel Publishing Company. Their warehouse had

caught on fire, destroying not only the building, but also their entire inventory which included all the unshipped copies of his new book *Valentino – The Unforgotten*. Still affected by the depression, The Wetzel Company couldn't financially survive the disaster and went bankrupt. Peterson's book was never republished. Since relatively few copies had been shipped out, it was indeed, a significant loss to the Valentino community. Peterson's first hand experiences at the mausoleum can never be underestimated. What he observed in those early years on a daily basis, was the laying of a foundation, and the beginnings of the Valentino cult. Through the years, the Peterson book remains even to this date, the most rare, and sought after of all the books written about Valentino. Right next to Natacha Rambova's 1927 book which was published only in England, (an inferior abridged paperback version was later published in the USA) Peterson's book is highly valued, and occupies a unique place, unlike any other book written on Valentino. After this devastating blow, it wasn't long before Peterson left his position at Hollywood Memorial Park Cemetery.

August 23, 1938: Aunt Teresa Werner, standing with arm on the ledge, visits Valentino's crypt. Joining her are kneeling left, Marybell Rathbun, Etta Fredrichson, Madeleine Thomas. Standing, Left, Teresa Werner, Katherine and Alice Kimbell.

1939 is arguably Hollywood's greatest year of achievement, the golden age of motion pictures. That year saw the release of *The Wizard of Oz, Gone With the Wind, Stagecoach, Dark Victory, Goodbye Mr. Chips, Wuthering Heights,* and *Mr. Smith Goes to Washington.* However on August 23rd, the films people were remembering had no color, had no sound. What they lacked in technical advancement was more than made up for in raw emotion, and passion for a bygone era. Those who gathered that year were not easily deterred. As reported "with trembling hands and tear stained cheeks, the women who still revere the memory of the screen's greatest lover paid floral tribute to him on the 13th anniversary of his death. All day they solemnly filed past Valentino's crypt in the Hollywood Cemetery Mausoleum, the women who, year after year have made a shrine of the actor's last resting place. Only one customary visitor was absent. The Woman In Black. Cemetery attendants reported that the mysterious and sorrowing woman, clad in a somber black dress and black veil, who paid annual visits to the crypt, did not make an appearance yesterday."

1940 – 1949

With the dawn of a new decade came unexpected new twists to the legend of the Valentino Memorial Services. Instead of winding down and fizzing out, the memorial services were growing, and heating up. Movie magazines of the day were filled with the latest insider gossip of stars such as Clark Gable, Deanna Durbin, and Judy Garland, to name a few. Yet, only one person from the silent era was still considered newsworthy, and shared valuable print space with the 'modern' stars. And that someone was none other than Rudolph Valentino. Articles such as *Rudy's Haunted House* and *The Night That I Slept in Rudy's Home,* or *Harry Carey Hunts for Ghosts* or *I was Valentino's Mystery Woman,* appeared regularly. The public never seemed to tire of Valentino.

As the memorial services unfolded for 1940, one didn't have long to wait for someone to take center stage. Roger Peterson had since left his position of almost 11 years, and Jack Fatland had taken his place as custodian of the mausoleum. Reporters were quick to notice that a Lady In Black "garbed entirely in black, veiled and wearing white rimmed sun glasses that looked more like goggles, arrived on the grounds as early at 6:00 a.m., one hour before the gates officially opened. She arrived by taxi, placed a basket of red roses and tuberoses at the mausoleum door and then lingered about the place. She readily posed for photographs but was reticent when efforts were made to learn her identity, which she refused to disclose." The photographers and reporters observed that she had disappeared before the actual doors to the mausoleum opened at 8:00 a.m., and had circled the building several times, without getting out, and then abruptly left. The newspaper went on to recall that "shortly before noon, Alberto Valentino, brother and only survivor of Rudy, placed two dozen roses at the base of the crypt. He remained in prayer for a few moments and as he walked out, he stopped to sign autographs. Cemetery officials estimated that approximately 500 persons passed in silence before Valentino's tomb." Ditra Flame could not attend that years memorial service and sent via messenger, a dome shaped basket of artificial flowers with a small sign with glued on gold foil letters stating 'Rudy from Ditra.' Those who chose to later peek at the card inside would find the following: "Dear Rudy, Sorry I could not bring this little token to your resting place, but I am ill, but you know we have not forgotten you." It was simply signed Ditra Flame. This would be the first time Ditra's name was publicly released to the press, and linked to that of the Lady In Black.

Prior to this, all of the so-called Ladies In Black were unified by their attire, and also the fact that none of them would give their names. They didn't seem to mind their photograph being taken, but they otherwise shunned the press. They didn't give interviews or say anything that would expose their identity, nor tell why they came to deeply mourn Valentino year after year. Ditra effectively broke ranks with all the other unnamed Ladies In Black and from this point forward would build momentum towards her claim to be the original. She had a very strong focus on who she was, and what she perceived her mission to be. It was her determination towards this effort that caused this year to be the turning point in the legend of the Lady In Black.

Jean Acker poses at the Valentino crypt on the day of the
Valentino Memorial August 23, 1940

The other big news that year was the unexpected arrival of Jean Acker. Papers reported that Jean "arrived at the cemetery in a limousine with her aunt, Mrs. Ann Acker of Philadelphia. They were followed by a crowd of onlookers into the mausoleum." Jean's appearance marked the only time one of Valentino's wives attended on the day of the memorial. Even how she was dressed made the papers. They stated that "Miss Acker, dressed in a beige suit, trim felt hat and accessories to match and a sable fur about her neck." With the crowd quietly watching, she placed her flowers, an arrangement of red carnations, at the base of his crypt and "remained in silence for a few moments and then took her leave. She made no attempt to shield her identity. She had no comment to make except to say that she wanted her visit to be as quiet as possible, explaining that she had called cemetery officials to learn if photographers had departed and inquired as to the size of the crowd." To the crowd's delight, Jean Acker courteously complied with requests to pose for photos of her standing in front of Valentino's crypt. As the day wound down, the mausoleum's bronze doors were slammed shut and locked at 5:00 p.m. sharp. The crowd, several who had come prepared with autograph books and cameras in hand, went home to wait for next years ceremony.

Alberto Valentino places flowers 1940

Unidentified woman places her flowers at the crypt

Newspapers inevitably reported on the activities that transpired at the memorial services. But in 1941 the Los Angeles Daily News got a jump-start, and on August 22nd ran an article with the heading "Tomorrow's the day to mourn for Valentino." Perhaps they were doing their part for public awareness to remind the local residents the day before the event. The article stated that "the fans who still remember, after 15 years will visit Hollywood Cemetery mausoleum tomorrow to pay their annual tribute of flowers at the crypt of Rudolph Valentino, once the undisputed great lover of the screen. Cemetery officials planned to station attendants at the crypt to handle the crowd of mourners, some of whom have been regular visitors since Valentino's death in 1926. Among them, it is expected, will be the customary two or three veiled women in black, arriving in expensive limousines. Originally there was only one Lady In Black." With the forewarning it was no wonder that the year's memorial would be well remembered. Not only was it the 15th anniversary of his passing, it marked the year that Ditra Flame arrived in person and declared herself as the original Lady In Black. The Los Angeles Herald Express papers, while printing Ditra's photo bowed before a floral arrangement at the crypt didn't buy into her story of being the original. They said "the veiled Lady In Black who for 15 years has kept an annual rendezvous at the crypt of Rudolph Valentino, in Hollywood Cemetery mausoleum did not appear early today on the 15th anniversary of the great sheik's death. But there was another Lady In Black there, unveiled, a lady poet and artist, and she knelt before the crypt and wept and prayed. And then she left a photograph of Valentino, framed in zinnias and roses and a poem which she had composed to the memory of the greatest of all the great lovers of the screen. The woman said her name was Ditra Flame and that she knew Valentino for six years before his death in 1926." They quoted her as saying "'But I am not the real woman in black' she said as she got back in her limousine and was driven away by a chauffeur." In her personal scrapbook Ditra pasted this newspaper clipping in, but was adamant that she hadn't given the quote about not being the original. In the margin of her scrapbook she wrote "Miss Flame did not make this statement to the press" and to further ease her frustration at being misquoted, she made a note that "No

Valentino Memorial Guild publicity to go to Herald Express." This article would begin Ditra's long acrimonious relationship with the press. She felt that through the years, she was invariably being misquoted or that the press was deliberately misconstruing her story.

Kneeling at the Valentino crypt is Ditra Flame. Ditra also presented to the cemetery the photograph of Valentino which rested on an easel covered with greenery and white mums. Circa August 23, 1941

Before Ditra got back in her limousine and departed, she told the crowd her version of the truth. It wasn't for love she declared, it was a mutual pact that she and Rudy had made. Several years later Ditra, fearing that someone else would falsely write her story, made a half-hearted attempt to write her memoirs. In her unpublished papers she wrote her version of how she came to know Valentino, and from that the legend of the Lady In Black was born. Ditra recalled "I saw Rudolph Valentino the first time when I was fourteen. He was living in a rooming house at 692 Valencia Street, in Los Angeles. Having spent some time in Mexico I mistook him for a Mexican and started my conversation in Spanish. The illusion was complete because he bubbled forth exuberantly. I felt dreadfully stupid because I lacked a command of the Spanish language and I lost my tongue in embarrassment. He said 'Sorellina, don't feel bad. I could speak only three words of English when I landed in America. I still don't speak well'. The barriers were down. The warmth of his understanding made me feel I had known him all my life. He left a lasting impression upon me which was evident when I was in a Pasadena hospital sometime later. I insisted I had to see Rodolfo Valentino, as he preferred to be called. As I look back now I know the nurses must have thought me a movie struck child in delirium. But up to that time I had not connected the dark Latin of my first meeting with any personality of the screen. That night I confided in the intern who had previously observed me kindly and he produced the pencil and paper upon which I wrote a note to Rudy, and he mailed it. The expression on the nurse's face was worth all my persistence when three days later Valentino actually appeared at the hospital and entered my room. 'What are you doing here, Sorellina?' he exclaimed. 'I have an abscess in my ear and the doctor thinks I will have to be operated upon,' I replied tearfully. 'No, no! That must not be', he excitedly paced the floor. 'But I feel terrible' I insisted. I must admit I wasn't lying. The pain was excruciating. In fact, I was so certain I was not long for this world that I bluntly told him so. Instead of laughing at me or saying anything trite in an attempt to raise my spirits, he became very serious. 'I do not think it is time for you to die, Sorellina. But if you do you will not be lonely because I will come every day to talk with you. Everything will be fine. I will bring you flowers and other people will too.' 'If there will be so many flowers how will I know which ones are from you?' I asked in all earnestness. 'Because my flowers will be different from the others. You will know. I will bring you a whole bush of oleanders. Remember, Sorellina?' Then he said something that was imprinted upon my mind for the remainder of my life. 'If I die before you do, I will expect something from you.' 'Oh yes, anything' I cried, hoping to please him. 'What will it be?' 'Very little, but it will mean very much to me. Just one red rose. Is it a promise?' I promised, and that moment I decided to live. His philosophy had worked the miracle because he had talked to me about what had been worrying me and made it seem all right."

The peace and tranquility at the 1941 memorial service was short lived. Four months later on December 7, 1941 the attack on Pearl Harbor catapulted the United States into WWII. Until the conclusion of the war in 1945 the current events of the day nudged the Valentino services off the pages of the press. While the tradition was continued, the annual affairs were generally kept low key. It would come to be regarded as a quiet time in the annals of history of the Valentino Memorial Service.

While the memorial services may have experienced a lull, there was nothing quiet about another rising claim to the ownership of the The Lady In Black title. This Lady In Black blatantly eclipsed Ditra Flame's earlier announcement. Not only did she release her name, as Ditra did, she did Ditra one better. She proclaimed that she had actually *married* Valentino in France the year before he died. And her claims became more outrageous. Subsequently she said that she had borne him a child who was then 19 and living in England.

Her name was Marion Benda Wilson. Marion, a Ziegfeld Follies star in the 1920's actually had known Rudolph Valentino and, as it turned out, old newspaper files revealed that Miss Wilson was with Valentino the night he was stricken. She had been his date the night he had gone to the infamous party hosted at the New York Park Avenue apartment of New York socialite Barclay Warburton. However on November 10, 1945, Marion Benda wasn't able to give the press this, or any other information. Her cousin, a young bodybuilder named Perry Combs had "identified Miss Wilson as the mysterious original Woman In Black, who yearly after Valentino's death left roses at his Hollywood Tomb." When pressed for information about the existence of a daughter of Valentino, Combs said "The marriage was not disclosed, because of the fear the disclosure would hurt the Italian screen star's romantic appeal. After Valentino died, he said she told me she just continued to keep it a secret." Despite her penchant for grabbing newspaper headlines, the troubled Marion had taken an overdose of sleeping pills, and it was her cousin Perry who found her "unconscious late yesterday at her oceanfront home. Fifty-seven sleeping tablets were missing from a bottle he said contained 63 tablets." Listed by police as a suicide attempt, Marion was held for psychiatric observation. As more of the lurid story unfolded, it was found out that she was the mysterious Lady In Black in 1940 who had worn the white sunglasses under her veil. Now, five years later she was fighting for her life. The fact that she actually knew and dated Valentino made her story carry more weight with the press. Valentino's manager George Ullman was quick to give a statement saying "Rudy dated her from time to time but I'm sure there was no marriage. As for her having a child by Rudy, there were 35 women who advanced that claim after he died." Alberto also released a joint statement with his son Jean Valentino. It all came as a surprise to them. They knew Rudy had known Marion but this was the first time they had heard of a marriage, and the papers duly noted that "Valentino's relatives scoff at secret wedding claim."

Ditra Flame was more determined than ever to prove her case over that of Marion Benda. As always, she took to her best line of defense - her typewriter. She began to type out explanation letters to members of her Valentino Memorial Guild. Perhaps dogging Ditra the most was the fact that Benda had known Valentino on a romantic level. It was undisputed that they had a few dates, including his last night on the town. At the same time, Ditra's claim was based on a long ago platonic, brother-sister type of bond. She well knew the wagging tongues of Valentino followers, as well as the press, would be allied against her, unless she could undoubtedly prove her case. She needed a knockout blow.

Much to her surprise as well as delight, Ditra's rescue came from none other than Marion herself. Just twenty-four hours after being rushed to the hospital, Marion was released, and found herself besieged by the press. They wanted to hear from her directly the claims made to the press by her cousin Perry Combs. The press noted that while she was "en route to the home of friends in North Hollywood, she denied an earlier report that she was the mysterious Lady In Black who annually placed roses on the tomb of Rudolph Valentino. However she did not deny nor confirm the tale that she was the third wife of the silent screen's great lover. 'I suggest you look up the records in New Jersey' she told newspaper men." The more the press began to dig the more they knew that Marion's story could not be true. At this point it was apparent to most that Marion was overcome by years of drug addiction, and failed marriages. It's certainly within a realm of possibility that she was harboring a tiny eternal flame of devotion to her friend, Rudolph Valentino. Who could blame her? And perhaps at this point in her life she came to believe her own story. It's certain that no one else did.

It was soon uncovered that although her *marriage* to Valentino never happened, Marion had in fact been wed to professional golfer Will Wise, and then to a German count, Baron Rupprecht von Boecklin, whom she lived with in Europe for almost ten years following their marriage. Her final marriage was to Doctor Blake Watson who worked at the St. John's Hospital in Santa Monica California. In light of such daunting and mounting evidence, it was clear there was no way Marion Benda could have been the original Lady In Black, appearing year after year. Although Marion herself had retracted any claim to the title, this comparison would haunt Ditra for the rest of her reign. Papers and movie magazines would continuously print their photographs next to each other with the caption "Rivals!" every time an article appeared about the legend of the Lady In Black, or if they were recapping that years memorial services. It didn't matter that it wasn't true, what mattered most that it was lurid; sensational. It was apparent that the public's appetite for Valentino lore was never ending.

Over the succeeding few years, the papers would be rife with sordid tales of Marion Benda being rushed in and out the hospital, all a succession of sleeping pill overdoses. The final time, as Irving Shullman's book *Valentino* stated, a "hearing was held in the hospital ward and Miss Benda presented a pathetic appearance. Without makeup, her dark red hair unkempt, and dressed in the ill-fitting nightgown that is hospital issue, she could hardly be visualized as one of the most famous of Ziegfeld's former showgirls. Judge Byrne read and evaluated the report of the hospital psychiatrists, weighed the findings and ordered Marion Benda committed to a mental institution, where she would be treated as a county ward." She was only 43 years old.

The confinement of Marion Benda left the field wide open for exploitation, and the opportunity wasn't lost on ever-determined Ditra Flame. In 1947 a reporter witnessed that "without fanfare, she arrived in a taxi shortly before 12:10 p.m. the hour of the romantic star's demise. She was unveiled. In her arms she carried a sizable bouquet of marigolds and asters." Ditra, although sincere of heart, was as theatrical as they come. Announcing to all that "I have been keeping the vigil since 1926" as she strolled into the mausoleum to place her offerings. "Once in the corridor where the body of Valentino rests, she reached into her ample purse and produced a mourner's veil. She draped it over her white hat, sat in a chair before the marble fronted vault and willingly posed for pictures. There was no dramatic demonstration of grief. 'I am president of the Hollywood Valentino Memorial Guild. We keep alive his memory.'" Once the press finished taking an ample amount of pictures for the next morning's editions, Ditra got up and left, telling those who remained that she was going home to write her book. Papers were quick to observe that "she was neither the first visitor to arrive nor was she the last. Earlier arrivals had left vases of red roses and a spray of gladiolas and carnations."

August 23, 1948, Ditra Flame pays her respects at the Valentino Memorial Service

The following year's memorial service wasn't much different from all the rest. The story began to repeat itself. Members of the media in vain hoped to catch two or more Ladies In Black visiting at the same time. In 1948 the memorial brought about a slight change in Ditra's arrival. While she arrived on time, this time there was no rented limousine. Newspapers told that "she arrived afoot, carrying an arm bouquet of asters and although the sun was hot, her pace was quick. She stopped outside for a sip of water at the fountain. Her dress was black. Her hat was black. Her accessories were black. In the book of sentimental keepsakes was a folded black veil. Once inside the mausoleum, she proceeded directly to the corridor where the body of Valentino rests. Already there were flowers in the two vases on the marble slab sealing the crypt, red dahlias. So, she arranged her bouquet in receptacles attached to neighboring vaults. There was no outburst of emotion. There was no thespic display other than posing for photographers. There was a brief conversation with newsmen about the contents of her scrapbook. She tarried only briefly, she had an appointment in town."

People wondered if she was the real deal. Another paper the same day reported in their headline that "Woman In Black Stirs Query In Visit to Valentino's Tomb." They openly wondered "Did the real Woman In Black visit the tomb of Rudolph Valentino? That question was pondered today as Hollywood wondered about a woman in black who appeared at the crypt yesterday at the stroke of noon. The woman who appeared to be middle aged and wore broad dark glasses, a heavy black veil and black clothing even to her stockings, gave her name as Ditra Flame, head of the Valentino Memorial Guild. She came to the Valentino crypt on foot, then kneeling in prayer for a few moments she placed the flowers in a vase beside the tomb and then hurried away. The quickness of her visit and her mode of transportation caused cemetery attendants and the crowd at the tomb to wonder whether she was the genuine Woman In Black. The latter heretofore has arrived in a black limousine, left her flowers before the crypt and spent many minutes in silent prayer."

When Ditra read the newspapers, which cast doubt on her credibility based on her mode of travel, she realized she had made a strategic mistake. She always read coverage of the events, and saved them all in her personal scrapbook, often correcting mistakes. But she now realized where she went wrong. In the earlier years, it was the 'mystery' of her identity that piqued peoples interest and gained extended media coverage. Since she had announced in 1941 who she was, that basic part of the legend was effectively destroyed. Now she found that even the mode of her transportation was observed. It was considered 'unbecoming' for the Lady In Black, who normally in years past had annually arrived in a chauffeured limousine, to come this year by bus, and hobble across the cemetery grounds on foot. Never one to repeat a bad entrance, Ditra managed to raise the money and hire a limousine, and in 1949 made the expected lavish arrival.

Other events were occurring in 1949 that kept Valentino's name in the forefront. Before they sold the estate, Gypsy and Gerald Buys on February 12th hosted a séance at Falcon Lair. Assisted by medium Carol McKinstry and a colorful personality named Rudolph Florentino. Florentino would prove to be a unique character in the Valentino circles. On July 6th it was reported that Gerald Buys committed suicide in San Francisco, apparently thinking he was terminally ill. The Buys' had recently sold Falcon Lair to a group who planed to present it as a prize for the best contribution to world peace in 1949. When an autopsy was later performed it showed no evidence of any cancer. Two days later on July 8th *Daily Variety* reported that a "battle looms between Edward Small and Jan Grippo, over Grippo's announcement that he will make a picture tagged *The Return of Valentino.*" The following week, on July 16th Louella Parsons announced in her daily column that Joseph Schenck was seeking the right to film the Valentino life story. Other tidbits in the news included the announcement on July 26th that the Secretary of State of California had "received papers today asking the incorporation of the Hollywood Rudolph Valentino Memorial Guild." By incorporating, Ditra was sending a signal to all, that her organization was "non profit benevolent and an educational involvement." But the most newsworthy event involved Marion Benda. Marion had been released from the institution and had gone right back to her self induced destruction. Papers declared that "for the fifth time in the last six years, according to police records, she was in a hospital suffering from an overdose of sleeping tablets." Marion's "physician rushed to her home at 5841 Carlton Way found her in a coma, in bed, in her blue and white pajamas and summoned police."

Just what was it that triggered Marion Benda's quest to self-destruct? She was the last woman to see Rudolph Valentino the night before his illness struck. Was she carrying some burden of internal guilt? Was there something she knew that the rest of the world didn't? It is no secret that rumors about how Valentino really died had made headlines shortly after his death. As late as the early 1990's Jean Valentino confided the opinion of his father, Alberto, stating he did not believe the official version of the story, but felt it was too late to take any type of action. Whatever the reason, Marion was re-institutionalized upon this fifth occurrence of attempted suicide.

Ditra arrives August 23, 1949

Ditra places her floral offering at the Valentino crypt.

At the 1949 services Ditra arrived shortly after noon in a chauffeur driven sedan. She wore a mourning dress and it was adorned with a thick black veiling with an added under-chin drape. Again, she knelt on the marble floor in front of his crypt and offered prayers. This time she wore on her left wrist a small Catholic crucifix made of dark wood on a strand of white rosary beads. Also this year the head of the English Valentino Memorial Guild made his first appearance at the Hollywood Valentino Memorial Services. Although their Valentino Guilds were not inter-linked other than in name, Ditra and the English Guild had communicated with each other and were on best of terms, for they were united in their goals.

1950-1959

With the passage of yet another decade, the dawn of the 1950's brought with it a renewed vigor and interest in the Valentino Memorial. People making the pilgrimage clamored this year more than ever to see the Lady In Black. It began to be apparent that her legend was beginning to have a drawing power of its own. Movie magazines were full of the latest news of Columbia Pictures' latest production of *Valentino,* which due to legal concerns was only loosely based on his life story. It starred the beautiful and radiant Eleanor Parker and introduced Anthony Dexter, the striking actor whom producer Edward Small had been grooming as Valentino's heir apparent. Although the film wouldn't be released until the following year, the publicity department at Columbia in true Hollywood fashion, worked overtime, feverishly pumping out news tidbits on all media fronts that would serve to stir up interest in the production.

At Hollywood Memorial Park, the services on August 23, 1950 were well attended by the public and the press, with Ditra Flame present once again to take center stage. Ditra insisted that "her film idol is spiritually alive" and those present witnessed her actions. "Followed by an entourage of newspaper reporters and cameramen, with an even dozen non working witnesses, she swept into the mausoleum, clad in a trailing black velvet gown, black velvet cap with an expanse of black veil streaming behind. At her throat was a tiny silver locket, bearing a photograph of Rudy, and at her side hung a silver crucifix on a long, silver chain. She removed two small bouquets placed in the urns flanking Rudy's marble-faced crypt. They had been left there at 8:30 a.m. by Rudy's brother, Alberto, according to cemetery staff members. She placed her own red roses in the urns, redistributed Albert's more humble floral offerings into the vases of the next crypt, occupied by June Mathis. Then she bowed her head in silent prayer for about 30 seconds. At the request of photographers she raised her head and presented her profile to the cameras." Then Ditra left the corridors of the mausoleum and took a stand outside, on the front steps.

Marion Benda dressed as the Lady In Black arrives at the mausoleum before it was opened for the 1950 Valentino Memorial. Along with her floral offering, she agreed to pose for the press before leaving.

78

Above: Ditra's limo arrives outside the mausoleum steps. Below:
Ditra gives an interview after depositing her flowers. Her Vice-President of
the Valentino Memorial Guild, George Harris, is standing at the left.

Ditra delivers her prepared speech on the front steps of the Cathedral Mausoleum
August 23, 1950

Throwing her veil back, she read a prepared statement that proclaimed "The first year, I came every day," she said. "You see he gave me a great deal of early training. He helped me enormously with my writing and especially with my thinking. Yes, I think Rudy is still alive, but definitely in the spirit, that is. I believe that the soul never dies, and that Rudy's soul continues to live and to be with us today. You can feel it here. I am sure of it." As the memorial service continued out in the open, on the front marble steps, Col. George J. Odgen, who was the chaplain for the Troupers of Hollywood, read his own eulogy. But most were there only to see the Lady In Black. After Mr. Odgen's remarks, Ditra stepped forward again, to read a poem by a dancer she hailed as "a person of prominence whose name I cannot divulge." At the poem's conclusion and the end of picture taking, she swept into the long black sedan which brought her there, and drove from the cemetery. When questioned by the press as to her opinion about the Columbia Pictures *Valentino*, which was reported to have wrapped principal photography on August 16, 1950, Ditra said that "The cast is doing a wonderful job, but the story is not the story of Rudy's life. If only they had used a script that was a true picture of his life, if only they had."

As Ditra Flame basked in her uncontested limelight, little did she know what the next year would bring forth. It would turn out to be a major milestone, as it marked the 25th anniversary of Rudolph Valentino's death. The planets all seemed to be aligned to make sure that 1951 was no ordinary year, and certainly one that none of the Valentino faithful would ever forget. The film *Valentino* would be released. Natacha Rambova would unwittingly find herself in the news, returning to the New York after a long absence and a failed second marriage. Irritated to find that her arrival fairly collided with the 25th anniversary, she flatly refused to give any statement or interviews about her time with Rudolph Valentino. Like Garbo, when it came to Valentino, Rambova wanted to be left alone.

August 23, 1951. On the 50th anniversary of Valentino's death, actress Patricia Medina
places a wreath at the crypt. Medina co-starred in the Columbia film *Valentino*, which was released
that same year

John Wayne Caley, 18, right, and Josee Metricks, 17, left, dressed in gaucho costumes
for the 50th anniversary at the Valentino Memorial Services on August 23,1951

On August 12th Ditra wrote to members of her guild that were planning on attending that they should "Be at the mausoleum, out on the steps about 11:45 a.m. August 23rd. Show me your card and get in our lines for the march to the crypt." As Ditra led her entourage of guild members down the marble halls, as she turned the corner approaching Rudy's grave, she was in for a shock. In addition to the throng of crowds, were newspapermen, and two teenagers named John Caley, 18, and Josee Metricks, 17. They were dressed in Gaucho costumes and willingly posed in front of Rudy's crypt to the delight of the reporters. Later Ditra witnessed Anthony Dexter and Patricia Medina, who were obviously there to promote the recently released Columbia Pictures movie *Valentino*. Although Ditra's arrival was expected, when she was compared to the outlandish publicity seekers in costumes, her appearance fell flat.

She had arraigned to have a portrait unveiled, of Rudy in his Sheik outfit, as well as a miniature bust of Rudy, which she planned to present both to the cemetery. It was after she placed her floral arrangement that things took an even more lively turn. "A worshipful crowd of tourists, publicity men and bobby soxers were kept jumping with the arrival of the Women n Black. A Swiss spiritualist, Amanda Tannarose gave a ten minute lecture on how she met Valentino ten years ago 'up there.' It seems she was introduced to him by a Persian poet, also dead. Then promptly at noon, Miss Flame arrived in a chauffeured limousine. She carried a bunch of red roses. These she placed in two vases flanking her idol's tomb. First she testily removed some flowers another Woman In Black had set there. She unveiled a life-size portrait of Valentino and a bronze bust. Both her gifts to the cemetery. Then Tony Dexter breezed in. 'He came right off the set of his next picture' a studio man yelled at reporters." Ditra posed in front of the crypt with Dexter and began to read a prepared "dramatic recitation of a self composed poem to Valentino's memory." A "pause following her declamation was broken by Amanda who obtained permission to sing *Sweet Bye and Bye* in a loud soprano voice." When Amanda asked permission to sing a second song, the request was denied. She sang anyways. "It was at this point that Ditra, solemnly standing in silent prayer, collapsed. As she was brought to, she asked for water but someone in the crowd unkindly said 'give her whiskey that's what she really wants.' A person brought the requested water, but things went from bad to worse, when someone drank the glass before it could reach Ditra. This brought on a violent tirade from Ditra, who cried, 'The doctor said I shouldn't come here today, but I had to come. It's my heart. I've been in bed for a year – there's too many people here. Make them go away, tell them to leave me alone, there's nothing more to see here.'" As the crowd was pushed back to give the distraught woman air, she moaned, 'I know they're saying this is a publicity stunt, but it's not.' She recovered from her faint rapidly, struggled ponderously to her feet. As she continued speaking, an argument broke out among spectators as to whether she was the bona fide Lady In Black." One bystander was interviewed and they said "She still gets billed annually as the 'mysterious Lady In Black' and she always lives up to the legend. But there's nothing very mysterious about her any more."

Ditra looks at Anthony Dexter as he places his flowers at the Valentino crypt on August 23, 1951. Dexter came from the set of his current film to attend the Valentino Memorial. He starred in the title role of the film *Valentino.*

The day that had begun on such a positive note had rapidly disintegrated into a public relations disaster. In one hours time Ditra had gone from upholding her title of Lady In Black to becoming a laughing stock. The next day's papers reported the spectacle: *Lady in Back Swoons at Crypt of Valentino, Lady in Black Faints Before Sheik's Tomb, Valentino 'Flame' Burns at Skeptics, Lady in Black Livens Up Solemnities By Crumbling In Faint At Valentino's Tomb*, and then *Shrieks, Sheiks, Shucks! Valentino Circus Has 25th Parade*. The articles under those headlines mocked Ditra, and accused her of insincerity. Ditra fired back to the *Los Angeles Mirror*, stating "I ask you in the name of decency, why send a reporter who has a bottle of printer's ink where his heart should be, to cover a solemn occasion? What could be gained for your paper by the article Valentino Circus has 25th Parade? Isn't the truth sensational enough? How could anyone who has access to the papers files come to such a conclusion that I have pulled an annual faint? I have never before fainted at Valentino's crypt, and would not have fainted this year had I not actually been ill. I dislike having the *Mirror* stamp me in print as an annual theatrical neurotic who seeks morbid publicity."

Ditra concluded her letter with "I suggest you refrain from printing any publicity on my activities, or the activities of my organization henceforth, unless you can print the truth." The editor placed his rebuttal under her letter, stating "If it wasn't a publicity stunt, why did a press agent pester us for a week to be sure we had a reporter and photographer on hand for your appearance?" Not all of the public was sympathetic to Ditra's claim of false reporting. One such letter came in from C.C. LaBelle who commended the paper's coverage by saying, "Your clever article on the Valentino Circus should put to shame Ditra Flame and the rest of the Ladies In Black who appeared. Why not come to your senses, Miss Flame, and realize what a spectacle you are making of yourself? Or won't you care? When she went into her annual faint and slipped gently and carefully to the stone floor, someone made a crack, and the fainting Flame cracked back. A person in a real faint is unable to wisecrack. It's plain that it's nothing but publicity. Let Valentino rest in peace!"

While Ditra was in a desperate fight to restore her credibility, another problem arose, and its serious, far reaching implications made Ditra nervous. Alberto and Jean Valentino had stepped forward, to express their extreme displeasure at the goings on at the crypt. Their interview was headlined *Tomb Circus Irks Valentino's Family* and *Valentino's Kin Decry Carnivals Held At Tomb*. The papers stated that "the morbidly emotional jags and the sideshow antics that take place annually at the tomb of Rudolph Valentino in Hollywood Cemetery may be halted by legal action, it was disclosed today. A request to end the disgraceful displays was made by Alberto Valentino and his son Jean. The father and son warned that if their request isn't complied with, legal steps will be taken to prevent a repetition of the slapstick such as was exhibited last Thursday on the 25th anniversary of the death of the great lover.

At that hero worshipping session the cast of characters included a few Women in Black, a couple of high school kids in desert costumes, a Swiss spiritualist, a hustling press agent with Tony Dexter, an actor, and a mob of bug eyed tourists. Each of the Women In Black insisted she was the original mystery woman who has been visiting the tomb for years. But none of them could match Ditra Flame when it came to emoting and swooning.

She upstaged the rest of the gang by chanting a syrupy sweet poem about Valentino's love lighting a thousand candles in her soul. The relatives finally rebelled today and said their attorneys have told them that they have grounds to take action against what they called 'degrading carnivals.' The elder Valentino, who is a studio film accountant, added 'We have always kept in the background. But even on the anniversaries of Rudy's death, the family has been unable to pay its respects at his tomb because it would involve us in the degrading carnivals that take place there.'" "Jean Valentino hastened to explain, however, that the family appreciates tributes paid in dignity by organizations and true friends, but that relatives were upset by the bad taste publicity stunts of others. It was so bad, said Jean that the family felt impelled to stay away from the tomb on the anniversary of the death." In her own defense, Ditra wrote in her scrapbook that "The press lives on controversy, makes big fight – sells lots of papers."

Ditra began her letter campaign again. Revealing her feelings about the Valentino family, on September 7, 1951 she wrote to Joan Soderlund and told her "I understand they have been very difficult to work with, regarding anything connected with Rudy. They started on George Ullman years ago and took him to court because they thought Rudy did not leave enough money for them. They could have worked on the *Valentino* script, I understand, but they were not satisfied with anything, so the studio made any kind of a picture to get out from under. I have a feeling they think I am making money on the Guild and they felt they should be entitled to some of it. I am just supposing because of their attitude. Also they feel that I am in the limelight because of the Valentino name and they can't take it. I can tell they don't want me in the limelight because of what Jean said to me over the phone.

After Columbia called me in to preview the picture, I called Jean Valentino, thinking he would like to hear a first hand report from me on the kind of picture the studio put out. He wasn't as interested in hearing about the picture as he was in showing his ire about the studios calling me instead of him. He said 'The studio should have called the Valentino family to see the picture before anyone else.' That was in February. I called him again the day after the 23rd of August. He hit the ceiling and said 'It was not your place to unveil the Valentino painting, it was my place if any unveiling was to be done.' He didn't ask me how my health was, he wasn't interested in that. He was only interested in his hurt pride apparently. My! They are certainly not anything like Rudy. No wonder he and Alberto never got along too well." When it came to her own defense, Ditra was never at loss for words. Only the week before, she had written Joan to explain her take on the unfolding disaster at the 25th anniversary. In retrospect, Ditra wrote that "I will try to forget the unfortunate things that have happened to me the past two weeks.

I never dreamed that because of a Hollywood press agent, who had no connection with me, and a Los Angeles newspaper noted for its smear sheet, would create such a humiliating situation for me. The records show that I have been going to Rudy's crypt for twenty-five years. There has not been a great to-do about my visit at the tomb until last year, August 23, 1950, a few months before the picture *Valentino* was to be released. It was then a Hollywood press agent (in some way connected with the studio making the *Valentino* picture) decided to 'use' me without my knowing it. He had known about my trip to the tomb and so he was 'on the spot' with props last Anniversary day. The props he had last August 23, 1950 were within keeping with the solemn occasion. He had gotten together a chaplain, and several other speakers to commemorate Rudy's 24th Anniversary. This year, the press agent was not so dignified, he brought Tony Dexter in makeup and Sheik costume. Naturally to some people it would look like a publicity stunt to bring Dexter who tried to look like Rudy. But here is the sad part as far as I am concerned. This publicity man called all the papers using my yearly pilgrimage as decoy so all the reporters and photographers would be sure to be at the tomb to photograph Tony Dexter. So, a certain paper decided I was in on the whole thing and wrote some very heart breaking publicity, building me up as a theatrical stooge who wanted publicity, and they wrote an article calling it 'Valentino Circus Has 25th Parade' and they made everything sound very phony. Naturally the Valentino family blamed me for the whole affair, and now after 25 years they have taken their wrath out on me because they couldn't fight Columbia Studios and stop the *Valentino* picture."

Hollywood Memorial Park had remained fairly neutral throughout the years in regards to the conduct at the Valentino Memorial Services. However after the adverse storm of negative publicity that followed the 1951 service, they decided they had to chart a course of action and take control. It is around this time that they sought the services of well-known Hollywood publicity man, Bud Testa. It would become Bud's job to annually oversee the memorial and coordinate everything in a dignified as possible manner. Up until this time, there was no structured service. Everyone knew it started at 12:10 p.m., the exact time Valentino had died (not making allowances for the east coast time difference). Most people who participated in the first twenty five years had read their prepared remarks in the alcove where Rudy lay, or at times even placed their flowers and gave their speech outside, on the mausoleum's front steps. Since there was no structured service, it was an 'anything goes' kind of atmosphere. Some people brought aluminum lawn chairs and parked themselves for a good portion of the day, in the corridor where Rudy lay in slumber. This assured them that they wouldn't miss a single thing. But now cemetery owner Jack Roth decided that Hollywood Memorial Park Cemetery had to at least make some attempt to restore order. With the hiring of Bud Testa, the whole style of the memorial changed. Now, chairs would be provided for the public, and there was an "official" service held in the main entrance hall. Selected speakers were there by invitation, and as an ensuing result the Valentino Memorial Services became much more subdued.

Still reeling over the bad press from the prior year, Ditra continued to explain her sincerity. On May 17,1952 she wrote to Frances Orton, to say "My life was dedicated to Rudy at the age of fourteen. He marked my life, of that you can be certain. There are people who think I have ulterior motives behind my activities for Valentino. Some think I have become rich by using his name. All of these things are idle rumors. And they are probably prompted by jealousy. So you see, when someone comes along like you with a heart full of understanding and sympathy I reach out to them across the miles and clasp their hand, and take them into my life and heart. I want no laurels for myself. I never did. My one thought is Rudolph Valentino. Wherever he is, I hope he knows and understands what a terrific battle I have put up in his behalf. Most people would laugh at that, believing him to be very dead. But I cannot believe that, because I believe in life after death, somewhere, somehow. Surely, this must be true, as the Master Jesus told us that there is such a thing as eternal life. I know the Valentino family are suing the studio. Also a spiritualist (Carol McKinstry) has written a book about Rudy saying he dictated it. Also, there are several rival Valentino clubs afoot. Poor Rudy. He certainly created a stir while he was living, but now, twenty six years later he is crating a cloudburst – that is, his name."

Just when it seemed things couldn't get any worse, three months after the anniversary fiasco, the Lady In Black name was in the headlines again. This time it had nothing to do with Ditra, although those who didn't know better associated it with her. The November 24, 1951 caption under a unflattering police station photo blared *The Screaming Lady In Black* with the following headline *Valentino Lady In Black Jailed on Narcotics Charge*. "Marion Wilson Benda the Lady In Black who each year decorates the crypt of Rudolph Valentino, screams and struggles with ambulance driver Bob Jarman after she was taken to Hollywood Receiving Hospital for an overdose of sleeping tablets. Later she was taken to Lincoln Heights jail on a narcotics charge." Her cousin, Perry Combs once again found her in her apartment with a nearly empty bottle of pills beside her, claiming she had been upset recently. It was apparent to all that she was clearly on a path of self-destruction that could only have one tragic conclusion. And so it came as no sudden shock, yet no less sad, when six days later the Friday headlines blared *Valentino Lady In Black Suicide*. With a large photo of Marion Benda, the article told how Marion finally succeeded after years of attempts. "Marion Benda was widely thought to be the mysterious Lady In Black who annually visited his tomb, was found dead today in the small Hollywood apartment where she lived alone. It was exactly a week ago tonight that the one time beauty was taken to Hollywood Receiving Hospital for treatment of an overdose of sleeping pills. That was the fifth time in six years, according to police records, that she and nearly succumbed to drugs. Today her body was found sprawled on the floor of her three-room apartment at 1825 North Wilcox Avenue by her cousin. In falling to the floor, police said she had suffered bad bruises and the cause off death was not immediately known. A quantity of pills was found on a nightstand, but the death was listed temporarily as possibly accidental." 'Of late more than ever, she talked of Valentino' her cousin Perry Combs declared.

Less than two weeks later, on December 12, 1951 Ditra wrote to Ellen Chambers and appeared less than sympathetic. She seemed glad for the curtain to come down on both Marion Benda as well as the year 1951. There is no doubt it had not been a good year for Ditra Flame. "Well, well. So the Lady In Black is DEAD! What a laugh, or it could be if the whole nasty mess wasn't so distasteful to me and the members of the Guild. What a way to kill the Valentino story! Headlines from coast to coast Valentino's Lady In Black was a dope addict, a mental case, and now a suicide. Somebody sure wants my hide. If they think that bad publicity will kill the guild just watch for next year's activities. My spirit shall live on, believe me! However the whole thing has given me an eerie feeling. Do you know that Marion lived just two blocks from me in Hollywood? I didn't know it until I read in the papers about her Hollywood address. Don't tell me I have been a stand-in for her for twenty-five years! For ten years after Rudy died she was in Europe so she never went to Rudy's crypt during that time unless I went for her. How weird. Both of us the same age, and with the same last name. Frankly I hope the fictitious Lady In Black stays dead, very dead!" Later in the letter, perhaps realizing her letter lacked compassion, she concluded with "I pray that Marion, wherever she is, finds a better reward if she has taken with her the stigma of the Lady In Black – the stigma I have carried for twenty five years, because I have been the one woman who has faithfully visited Rudy's crypt for that length of time. Yes the stigma of hatred and jealousy, may it now also die."

In a letter dated June 20, 1952 Ditra wrote to Frances again and answered the question put before her as to why she chose to reveal her identity. Ditra explained that "For many years I kept my identity a secret because I did not want the press to spread my name around, and I did not go to his crypt for publicity but to keep a sentimental tryst with remembrance. However, about ten years ago the rumor got started that a jealous woman from Rudy's harem had thrown acid in my face and marred my features. Well, that was too much for me, it was then I lifted my veil, and that has been a long time. Ever since then the newspapers have carried pictures of me with veil lifted, and printed my name. I am the only woman who has kept the tryst in black at Rudy's crypt for twenty-five years. I have plenty of proof of that, regardless of the rumor stories by jealous people, and including one Marion Benda who recently committed suicide. She was a narcotic addict, I think I told you, and when the police would take her in to jail she started screaming she was the Lady In Black. Well, we do not have to worry about her anymore."

The release of Columbia Pictures' *Valentino* awakened many young girls who weren't alive in Rudy's day, to his magnetic screen personality. Several made their way to becoming members of Ditra's Valentino Guild. One person was a young girl named Helen Affeidt, who lived in Washington State. She eagerly exchanged letters with Ditra and gave her any bit of news that she heard from rival clubs. On June 13, 1952 she provided a tidbit that troubled Ditra Flame. Stating that a girl from the Valentino Flappers club named Myrna wrote to her, Helen told Ditra that Myrna "Says she doubts if you'll partake in the services at Rudy's tomb, since his family are trying to fix it so you can't. Is his family jealous or what?" Within four days, Ditra fired off a three-page letter. She asked Helen to "Find out where Myrna got the information that the Valentino family are trying to fix it so I will not appear this August 23rd. This is most important, as it is all news to me. Why should they start fixing it twenty-six years later? Though I do know from other sources that they are on the jealous side because I have had so much publicity the last three years. I do not know the Valentino family and I do not want to know them. They are very unlike Rudy. All they can think of is suing people to get money." Ditra closed her letter repeating the urgency of her message, stating "Please get the above information as I want to be ready for anything that might happen at the tomb ahead of time. This is a free country, I do not see what they think they can do to keep me from visiting a grave in a public cemetery. If they try anything, they will get a lot of publicity, and that is probably what they are after."

Prior to receiving Helen's letter Ditra had trouble with yet another overzealous Valentino follower. A lady named Mary Hammin who daily stayed beside

Valentino's crypt and questioned any and all who stopped by. She did not like Ditra and was freely saying such to anyone who stopped by the crypt.

Unfortunately, Mary's opinions were formed by the exaggerated stories she had read, as well as heard from rival clubs. Ditra decided a proper course of action would be to plead her case right to the top. With the memorial services just around the corner, she couldn't afford to take any chances. On May 20, 1952 she wrote to Hollywood Memorial Park Cemetery owner Jack Roth. The main focus of her letter was to draw attention to Mary Hammin's bizarre activities at the cemetery. Ditra told Mr. Roth that "I have sent flowers to Mr. Valentino's crypt by my Guild members several times in the past year. I understand from a reliable source (the letters are in my files) that a Mary Hammin has removed all flowers from Mr. Valentino's crypt bearing my name and that of the Valentino Guild.

According to Miss Hammin's conversation, she has decided that no one can place flowers on Rudy's crypt but herself. I am sickened by the reports of her malicious defamation of my name and organization and her attempt to impress the people who happen to run into her at the crypt. If I knew her address my attorney would write to her and tell her we are prepared to start suit on her unless she stops her ugly rumors. However, that would only give her more importance and the publicity she seeks. Personally, I think Miss Hammin's speech and actions are entirely out of bounds especially in a cemetery. I am so sorry that Miss Hammin feels such jealousy toward the many people who would like to place a memory offering on Mr. Valentino's crypt. After all, Rudolph Valentino does not belong to any one person. He belongs to everyone. It seems a pity our members and friends cannot place flowers on his crypt without the stooge of a certain group calling themselves the Rudolph Valentino Memorial Club of Hollywood, removing them. I have had so many inquiries from interested people all over the world for information about the place where Rudy is buried, and of course they want specific directions how to get there when coming to California. I am wondering if it is wise to give these people information with a watch dog at the crypt." Ditra closed her letter with "I hope that you in some way, will be instrumental in promoting goodwill at the crypt of Mr. Valentino."

Jack Roth mulled over Ditra's letter for a few days and then shared it with his new publicity man, Bud Testa. On July 24, 1952 Bud wrote Ditra and totally side-stepped her plea about the Mary Hammin situation, only saying "Mr. Roth showed me your letter, and I am glad to see that you are in good heath again. Please let me know if you are planning to be present again on August 23 for Rudolph Valentino's anniversary." Clearly the cemetery was wanting to see what each side had in the works. Ditra realized that if the Valentino family was involved it could be another disaster. She had no intention of repeating last years mistakes. The thing she feared the most was that as she departed her limousine, and made her way up the steps of the mausoleum, that a court process server would present her with a court mandated restraining order on behalf of the Valentino family. She knew this would be the death knell to her legitimacy, should it occur.

So, not wanting her 'fingerprints' on it, she directed the Executive Secretary of her Guild, George A. Harris, to test the waters. Seeing that her earlier letter was turned over to Bud Testa, Ditra realized he was the man who held the answers. So, two days after Bud Testa's letter, on July 26, 1952, George Harris wrote to Bud saying "Miss Flame has turned your letter of July 24th over to the Board of Trustees of the Rudolph Valentino Guild for their consideration. We wish to advise that the Rudolph Valentino Guild is planning to present floral offerings at the Valentino crypt August 23rd at noon. However, the Board of Trustees of the Guild is debating as to whether they will permit Miss Flame to appear at the Valentino crypt this year due to the Valentino family's attitude of last year, and the criticism from the newspapers. Since you have open sesame to the Hollywood Cemetery, perhaps you have heard whether or not the Valentino family intends to carry out their threat to serve restraining papers on Miss Flame to bar her from the crypt this year. We would appreciate any information regarding this matter. Also, we would like to know what type of a program you have planned for the activities at the Valentino crypt. Your reply could influence the decision of the

Board of Trustees of the Rudolph Valentino Guild." It was clear, calculated, strategic maneuver to force the Valentino family to show their hand.

Anyone who knew Ditra knew that a team of wild horses couldn't keep her from appearing at the annual memorial services. Certainly the committee members of her own Guild held no power over her, as they did her bidding. On August 9, 1952, Bud Testa replied to George Harris' letter, stating that "I have not heard anything from the Valentino family, and doubt if I or the Cemetery will, as the cemetery is open to the public, and they cannot bar people from entering it." Ditra was relieved to a great extent to find out that it had only been a threat, and that the family had not pressed the issue to the point of seeking legal action. With that major worry out of the way, Ditra geared up for yet another year. Now Ditra pressured the cemetery for security to be present at the crypt. With the knowledge of the previous years 'carnival', there was little else they could do, but comply with her wishes, if they wanted to appear serious in bringing order to the Valentino Memorial Services.

Ditra was ecstatic when notified by Bud Testa that the cemetery would post a guard at the Valentino crypt on the day of the memorial. On August 4, 1952 just a mere nineteen days before the service, she again wrote to cemetery owner Jack Roth. "Mr. Testa has informed me that you will place a guard at Valentino's crypt August 23rd. Words cannot express my appreciation for your kind consideration. I hope there will not be a repetition of the 'carnival' of last year for which I and the Valentino Guild were in no way responsible. The trustees of the Valentino Guild do not feel that the solemnity of the anniversary should be placed in an unfavorable light by allowing people in theatrical costumes to appear at the Valentino crypt. I am certain that Rudy would have had more respect for the departed than to appear in such a manner. It has always been my desire that the Valentino anniversary be held in reverence and solemnity as fitting tribute to Valentino's artistry and fame. Our contribution to his memory should be in keeping with his contributions to the cultural development of our nation and the world nations. We have tried to keep it this way but during the past few years others have taken it upon themselves to mutilate our endeavors for the screen's greatest personality."

As delighted as Ditra was that the cemetery was stationing a guard at the crypt, threatening letters continued to pour in. She decided she needed a personal bodyguard, and she had George Harris draft a letter to the Hollywood Detective Agency located at 7556 Hollywood Blvd. He wrote "Miss Flame, President of the Rudolph Valentino Guild has asked me to write to you regarding a body guard to accompany her to the Hollywood Cemetery August 23rd, at noon. Unfortunately, Miss Flame has received threatening letters, and crank letters, probably prompted by jealousy. Last year there was an attempt at blackmail." Harris proceeded to explain what Ditra was up against. Stating "Mary Hammin haunts Valentino's crypt at the Hollywood Cemetery and tells everyone who comes there malicious lies about Miss Flame and her organization. Last year she attacked Miss Flame on the cemetery grounds. The forgoing is the reason we want a bodyguard for Miss Flame. To keep order at the crypt in case anyone tries to disturb the peace while she is making her yearly pilgrimage to Valentino's crypt with her floral tribute. Your services would be necessary for an hour. 11:45 a.m. to 12:45 p.m. Please let me know your fee for this service."

The agency wrote back to inform the Guild that they would be glad to take on the assignment, but they had a one-day minimum fee. This put a crimp in the Guild's operating budget. They quickly put their heads together and felt that perhaps they could squeeze a little more value out of the one day they hired the bodyguard. On August 11, 1952 Ditra herself wrote to H.L. Von Wittenburg, head of the agency. She inquired that "There are a few questions I would like answered. Since the fee of twenty-five dollars applies to a full day, I am wondering if you would write two letters for me. One letter goes to the Mary Hammin who has been causing so much trouble for me, the other to another woman in the cast who has been writing malicious letters about me. It might carry more weight if said letters came from a detective rather than an attorney." Ever frugal, Ditra wrapped up her letter with another question. "Can you furnish a black car for me to ride to the cemetery in, with the bodyguard? I could not very well pay for a motor delivery and detective at this time, as we have gone to quite a lot of expense for floral tributes and other details." Mr. Von Wittenburg complied and the deal was set.

Meanwhile, George Harris answered Bud Testa's letter on August 13, 1952 by saying "Since you are handling news publicity we would appreciate it very much if you would see to it the *Mirror* does not get any publicity on Ditra Flame. Last year, simply because you mentioned she would be at the crypt, there was much in the *Mirror* about her having a publicity agent that haunted their office to be sure their newsman would be on the spot for her arrival. All the other papers are OK as far as we are concerned." Mr. Harris said what everyone else already knew, and decided to take it a step further when he asked Bud that "Miss Flame feels that there is no longer a necessity to be played up by the press as the mysterious Lady In Black, since she has had so much publicity in the past, and her identity has long been made public." The service on August 23, 1952 fell on a Saturday. Ever the publicity agent, Bud Testa wired a telegram to the Valentino Guild on August 18, 1952 telling her that he had been notified that "Newspaper deadlines for pictures are before noon on Saturdays, suggest you have Ditra appear at 10 a.m. Call me immediately if this can be arranged."

To her credit, as well as proof that she wasn't just wanting to see herself getting publicity in the papers, Ditra brushed aside Bud Testa's suggestion to appear two hours earlier, so that reporters could make their weekend photo deadline. The official time was 12:10 p.m., and 12:10 p.m. it would be. At the designated time, Ditra made her way down the now familiar path of marble flooring, to the Valentino crypt. The reporters were all anxious to see what would transpire, and their wait was well rewarded. "With her face bared but dressed in the deepest mourning, the usual Lady In Black yesterday led the memorial services for Rudolph Valentino at Hollywood Cemetery on the 26th anniversary of his death." The *Los Angeles Times* noted that "the Lady In Black was there, Ditra Flame, bearing roses to the crypt. This time she was joined by the Lady In White. A woman of mystery who calls herself Amanda, a name she says, given her in the eleventh century by Omar Khayyam, the great Persian poet. Then Amanda told of a spiritual visit from Valentino at 7:00 a.m. on Friday. His message to Amanda asked that peace be proclaimed among nations, ending with 'Farewell, my friends – peace prevail within your souls.'" To Ditra, the mysterious Lady In White was no mystery at all. She was the same Amanda Tannarose, who at the previous year's memorial had called herself a Swiss singer and spiritualist, who had sang *In the Sweet Bye and Bye*. Ditra had no sense of humor regarding someone she felt so irreverent, and placed her in the same category of others who made it their habit to loiter around the crypt throughout the year. Rudolph Florentino, Mary Hammin, Connie King, and a handful of others would continue to be a source of annoyance to Ditra.

The papers also noticed the change in security at the services, stating "in brief quiet services held in a corner of the mausoleum, behind a guard of three sheriff's deputies" who were there to protect not only the dignity of the occasion but to also assist in keeping Ditra safe from those who had threatened her well being. Under protection, Ditra got bold and gave her oft-told story, telling the crowd that "I was the original Lady In Black, and for many years I came to mourn quietly." Then with an obvious glare at Amanda, the 'Lady In White,' in a deliberately louder voice, she continued "Then a lot of phonies started coming." As she made her exit Ditra did a quick head count and realized that there were barely fifty people attending. Of course, several had come and gone throughout the day, but she was dismayed to see such a lackluster crowd. Much had happened to erode interest in the Valentino Memorial Service.

A ground swell of negative publicity resulting from the previous year's 'fainting' had turned many people off, as they assumed it was only a self serving publicity stunt. Also, with the death of Marion Benda by an overdose of sleeping pills, again the Lady In Black's name was placed in a negative light in the press. The Valentino family's decision to take their displeasure public, as they cried out against the 'carnivals' held at Rudolph's crypt also contributed to the erosion of support and interest. The highly fictionalized film *Valentino*, released by Columbia Pictures flopped at the box office, and failed to generate an extended renewal of interest in the real Valentino. The ranks of the faithful were thinning out. Due to all those things as well as death, and old age, the wind of change was clearly in the air. A brand new idol, called the King of rock and roll, Elvis Presley was taking the nation by storm. The Valentino Memorial, although it was destined to continue, was going through rough times.

After the memorial, Helen Tull wrote to notify Ditra of Mary's Hammin's actions. She told how "Mary Hammin moved your flowers after you left and put hers in, then she took part of hers out and made room for Florentino to put his in! Poor Rudy. I saw Mary yesterday at the crypt. It takes her about two hours to get her flowers fixed to suit her. She can always find time to tell people all about Rudy. She can only afford the cheapest flowers and she keeps taking them back outside and cutting the stems off a little more. She had on a new black coat, and she told me before that she did not intend to wear black any more, she was afraid that Alberto would not like it. She still has hopes of getting to know that family. She even goes out behind the mausoleum and picks up any scraps of paper or dead leaves. She waits around the cemetery hoping to see Alberto, she did see him at one time, months ago, when he brought flowers. She told him she kept flowers there at all times, and of course he thanked her. She tries to see the nephew (Jean) but he told her to 'forget the past.' She made complaints of you at the office at the cemetery and also had other people calling there with complaints."

At this point Ditra knew things could easily spin out of control again. She felt people lumped her into the same category as the crackpot Swiss spiritualist, Amanda, Rudolph Florentino, Connie King and Mary Hammin. Later in another letter Helen Tull revealed "I was out to the crypt on Decoration Day and there were ladies there telling other women all about the roses you place on Rudy's crypt on his anniversary. Mary was there and heard the women talking and did she look funny. Say here is a gruesome twosome. Connie King went to the Frank E. Campbell undertaking parlor in New York and demanded to see the table where Rudy was embalmed. She asked them what they did with his blood. When told they put it down the sewer drain, she told them they should have put it in small bottles and the women would have drank it." Ditra's wrote back to say that the incident "Really gave me a jolt."

Looking back on the memorial service, on January 20, 1953, Ditra wrote to Pat Goldman and reflected that "The Valentino Memorial Services were lovely, and there was a large crowd there. No nonsense like 1950 and 1951. I had police stationed there this time to see that no one got out of line. I guess I told you that the publicity was quiet, as the Saturday deadline is 10 a.m. and I refused to appear earlier for their convenience. However, what they did say about us was very dignified, and I appreciated that, for a change."

Following the 28th memorial service in 1953, the *Los Angeles Times* published their story. They showed a photograph of Ditra, with her veil drawn down over her face, solemnly standing in front of Rudy's crypt. Yet, the telltale sign of tiredness was evident by what they chose as their headline. *Forgotten? Few Honor Memory of Valentino*. They told that "only a handful of the faithful and the curious yesterday joined Ditra Flame, the perennial Lady In Black. She was dressed in black and a full black veil concealed her face. She carried two dozen red roses. She walked quickly through the marble halls to the alcove where the body of the great screen idol rests in his crypt. An entourage of reporters and photographers followed her. Behind them a crowd of 20 or 30 mourners and spectators brought up the rear. Repeating the ritual she has performed for 27 years, the Lady In Black swiftly plucked the long stemmed roses from the bouquets and placed them in twin urns on the crypt. Then she stepped back beneath the window of colored glass. 'Ladies and Gentlemen, she began, 'We are here to honor the memory of a great artist.' Miss Flame read firmly from a prepared eulogy held in an open book. A rosary dangled from her left wrist. Also among the mourners was James Kirkwood, who was already an idol of the silent screen when Valentino burst upon the world. He stepped forward to place a wreath on the crypt, and spoke a few words in behalf of the Masquers, and Belle Martell, representing the Troupers."

Ditra's archenemy of the press, the *Mirror*, from whom she had tried to withhold press releases, was among the reporters. True to form, their slant on the

101

services tended to mock Ditra. They stated that the memorial was a "dull affair" and were quick to mention that "it was dull when compared with past performances. And the house was slimmer." The *Mirror* stated that "instead of the usual half dozen dolls in widow's weeds, waiting in anguish while they upstaged each other, the only woman in black to show up at Hollywood Cemetery yesterday was Ditra Flame.

No swoons, no cases of vapors, the usual mob had dwindled to a handful." They told of the participation of James Kirkwood and that he had told the crowd that he thought Valentino was aware, and said "I think he knows we're here." Belle Martell after making her presentation on behalf of the Troupers told the crowd that "Some day we will all meet again in his dream room upstairs." Then, raising her finger in the air, she smiled and in closing spoke her trademark phrase: "Until next year!" And so, another year came to a close on a disappointing note. While the press, outside of the *Mirror*, was generally respectful, the truth of the matter was, the original "players" were fading away, and no fresh new ones were there to carry on. So, it was up to Ditra to make a decision on her future involvement. One of Ditra's favorite sayings was "Its time to change the script." This time, it was aimed towards herself.

Determined to go out in style, she waited until the following year to make a formal announcement about the new direction in her life. All the while, her dedication to Rudolph Valentino never wavered, but she felt she could no longer solely bear the brunt of the burden of keeping his memory alive. In a letter she wrote to Helen Affeidt shortly before she announced her decision, she made her final attempt to explain what she had gone through over the years. As far as claims that she had reaped financial gain through her Guild were concerned, Ditra scoffed. "As to the money involved, that could be a laugh if it weren't so tragic. Through the years I have spent my own money to carry on the Guild. I have often gone without things I needed myself, to keep the fires burning for Rudy. That is a long, sad story. I have had so much humiliation already that now I consider the source, and I carry on anyway. I shall continue to do so. Believe me, when I say I have never made a dime from the Valentino name, nor the Valentino Guild.

The five dollars a year that people send in doesn't even pay for postage stamps due to the tremendous correspondence people expect from me." Ditra, caught up in her self examination, concluded the letter to Helen with "I feel in my heart you really understand me and my inner feelings about Rudy, and what I have tried to do to keep his name alive all these years. I have endured endless torture, but it has all been torture from worldly people who cannot understand a person with higher aspirations than that of gathering money. A mess of pottage that they cannot take with them, when they leave this world."

This was the first glimpse of the new spiritual side of Ditra. It would be on August 23, 1954 that she would let everyone else in on her newfound faith, based on her recent conversion to Christianity. The many different headlines told the whole story. *Lady In Black Now Lady In White, Ditra Flame Quits Lady In Black Role, Lady In Black in Last Visit to Valentino Tomb, Woman In Black pays Last Homage to Valentino, Sheik's Lady In Black Appears in White.* As reported by the press "After 28 years – the end. Never again will the Lady In Black sorrow at the crypt of Rudolph Valentino, film star of the silent era. Never again will she walk through the echoing corridor of the Hollywood Mausoleum. Never again will she dispose the red roses in a message of remembrance. Miss Flame appeared yesterday, not in black, but in white, with a blue cape draped over her right shoulder, she bore a basket of red roses carrying the imprint of the Rose of Sharon Evangelical Ministry." Another paper played with the words, and declared "the Woman In Black didn't show today, but a Lady In White took advantage of her absence. While scores of the dashing actor's friends and fans stood respectfully near the crypt in the Hollywood Memorial Park Cemetery, the woman, wearing a white gown, white veil and white gloves, busied herself placing photographs of the Latin lover of the screen around the crypt." "'I am Amanda of the Eternal Life Association,' she told newspapermen. 'I saw, and talked to Rudolph last Friday night. He visits me regularly but not too often, he is busy studying for his reincarnation.'" Amanda mentioned what message Valentino had given to her, to pass along to all the earthly mortals. She said he had told her 'Be you perfect in your heart.'

Belle Martell, left, James Kirkwood, Ditra Flame, all listen as George Harris reads Ditra's introduction at the Valentino Memorial August 23, 1954, the day she announced her departure from the annual ceremonies.

"James Kirkwood, himself a film star during the Valentino era, placed a wreath beside the Valentino crypt as the representative of the Masquers Club, Hollywood theatrical organization, and delivered a brief and serious eulogy extolling the art and virtues of the first actor to bring the surge and swing of he-man sex to the screen. Belle Martell represented the Troupers, another theatrical organization." Miss Flame was accompanied by George A. Harris, vice-president of the Hollywood Valentino Memorial Guild, who said that the occasion of the yearly visit to the crypt had become tarnished. The original purpose had become smothered in the stories of sensational writers. After full consideration, he said, Miss Flame had surrendered her life to God and she stood before the little group dedicated to the Rose of Sharon Evangelical Ministry. When Ditra spoke she said "My appearing at the crypt seems to have become a symbol for the dead rather than the living."

And so, the end of an era had come. Ditra summed up her feelings in a long, reflective letter written to Philomena Rose Miller on October 1, 1954. Up front about her feelings, Ditra stated that "Surely you must know I must have had good reason to stop being the Lady In Black. I hope to write a book one day about all

104

my experiences since 1926, Valentino's death, and set forth in the book the truth about my association with Rudy and also what happened to me since his death. You see, from the seed of sympathy and love, and esteem, I held for Rudy, as well as the keeping of a promise to see that he would always be remembered with red roses, sprang the sensational seeds and thistles strewn by the press. What was once a lovely act grew into a hideous over-grown vine that choked out the sweet early memories of a man who was my friend and big brother. Year by year as it grew, other people, seeking publicity came into the picture. People who had no sense of loyalty to Rudy, they never knew him.

They were strange, unreal personalities, jealous of my fame and so they did everything they could possibly do to make me look ridiculous in the eyes of the public. Their names would be linked with mine because they were present at the annual memorial services for Rudy, and even though I did not know these people personally, the public believed me to be the one who had them at the crypt. Thus, my name became associated with spiritualists, publicity seekers, and crackpots in general. The final blow came from time to time when Marion Benda got into the papers, about two years before her death. Marion had been a Follies beauty back in the 1920's and she happened to be at the last party Valentino attended in New York. Since Rudy was unattached before his death when he died, the press looked for a sensational love interest in his life. The love interest between Rudy and Pola Negri had long since died a natural death, so the press looked around for something different. Marion's picture was carried in the papers as the last date that Rudy had, because she was a Follies girl. It made good reading as far as the public was concerned.

Soon after Rudy died, Marion married a Count and went to live in Europe. She lived there for ten years. For ten years while Marion was in Europe, I was going as the veiled Lady to Valentino's tomb. So, Marion could never have been associated with the title of the Lady In Black. Yet, in later years, Marion became a narcotic addict, and when the police took her in she screamed to the press that she was the Lady In Black. One morning the newspaper, in big bold, and very black headlines this appeared: *Lady In Black, Narcotic Addict, Tries Suicide.* You can imagine how I felt. I knew the public would associate those headlines with me, and so they did. For I received many letters condemning me for my acts, and many letters were very cruelly written 'Why didn't you kill yourself off, you old bag. You are not fit to associate with decent people anyway.'

A group of people in Philadelphia threatened to break me and my association with the Valentino Guild, saying I was an unfit person to be the head of the organization, which I founded in 1926. They tried to cause me no end of trouble, but of course, they got nowhere legally. Many other things happened too numerous to mention here. When Marion finally did commit suicide, the headline read: *Lady In Black Commits Suicide.* That did it! People from all over the country and out of this country sent in telegrams to the Guild, some sorry for my death, others glad for my death. Flowers were sent for my funeral, and so on. It was horrible! The papers finally ran a small retraction in such fine print, few people ever had a chance to read it. Reporters are paid to write sensational stories. When they wrote up the story on Marion they made it sensational to the hilt, then the last paragraph read, 'to the last, Marion denied being the real Lady In Black.' But no one ever read the last paragraph because of all the black, sordid, sensational news that came before the end. That is the way reporters work, but the public does not know the methods used by the press in presenting a 'story.' Most people believe what they read in the paper about famous personalities. More is the pity. This is only one of hundreds of situations in which I found myself because I was associated with the famous name of Valentino, and because many years ago the press had given me the title of 'The Lady In Black'.

Please, tell your Aunt Clara that no one could ever be as shocked at my retirement than I have been, through the years with heartbreaking situations caused by the public and the press alike. Somehow, in my heart, Philomena, I knew you would understand. No one can ever keep me from praying for Rudy, or thinking about him, or from sending roses to his resting-place. But now, I can do all this without the world judging my motives. Since few people understood my vigil at Rudy's crypt, I would rather pay my respects to Rudy in quiet, and work for the Kingdom of God openly." And in final thought Ditra said that "I think that I have talked quite enough for this time. Enclosed please find your membership card, life membership in the Valentino Guild. I thought you would like to have it, to keep always."

It wasn't often that one found Ditra in such a reflective and forthright mood. Perhaps she herself sensed the end of an era, no doubt she had her own regrets and misgivings, but what was done, was done. In his 1967 book Irving Shulman said it best when he wrote of Ditra's departure "She retired from the scene, leaving the field wide to fakes, starlets and kooks. After Ditra's farewell appearance, the Valentino Memorial Services lost their zing; the pageantry and pathos of former years had departed with her." And so, an important chapter in the memorial services had drawn to a close. There is no way one can under-value Ditra's contribution in perpetuating the memory of Rudolph Valentino. The truth of the matter is the legend of the Lady In Black was a pivotal force in keeping the press coming back year after year. She persevered whether the public was for her, or against her. Her goals were uncomplicated and she felt that her mission had been completed. To Ditra, she had fulfilled a commitment to a very dear friend that dated back to Rudy's visit to her hospital bed in 1920. The Valentino Memorial Services would never, even to this day, regain the flavor that Ditra brought with her, on August 23rd of every year. Without a doubt, Ditra Flame would be missed.

Among Ditra's detractors, several skeptical people wondered if Ditra would make good on her pledge to shun the next year's services. They only had to wait until August 23, 1955 to get their answer. The newspaper headlines told it all. *Lady In Black Shuns Valentino Rites, Lady In Black Missing at Valentino Ceremony, Lady In Black Fails to Show at Valentino Rite.* Now, without her having placed a single footstep down the marble corridors, Ditra was again the focus of the 1955 Valentino Memorial Services.

Crowds jam the Valentino crypt alcove. Security guard can be seen at rear center. Circa 1955

Assisted by Belle Martell, right, James Kirkwood places a floral display at
the Valentino crypt on the August 23, 1955 Valentino Memorial Service.

Papers were quick to note her absence, stating that "the 29th anniversary of Rudolph Valentino's death was duly observed yesterday by about 100 mourners who assembled before his crypt at the Hollywood Mausoleum. They heard eulogies to the great screen lover of yesteryear voiced by James Kirkwood and Belle Martell, both former stars and friends of Valentino. And everybody was on the lookout for the Lady In Black, Ditra Flame, who, for years, had placed roses before the crypt and who, shortly after the death of Valentino, founded the Rudolph Valentino Guild Inc. But she kept the promise she made last year. She didn't show up. At last year's observance, when she suddenly became a Lady In White, in the uniform of the Rose of Sharon Evangelical Ministry, Miss Flame announced she had found God, was dedicated to serving the living and through with weeping for the dead. There was no other representative of the Valentino Guild present. George A. Harris, announced that members of the Guild have chosen a less spectacular day than August 23rd for their annual tribute. The mourners and curious began gathering at the crypt at 11 a.m. in anticipation of the noon memorial services. They heard Kirkwood, representing the Masquers, proclaim that they were not there to mourn Valentino, but to rejoice in the memory of association with him. After reciting the lengthy poem, *I Shall Not Pass This Way Again* Kirkwood voiced a few reminiscences of his friendship with Valentino. Belle Martell, representing the Troupers and the Benevolent Thespians, eulogized Valentino as a symbol of romance, a dashing, handsome hero who brought storybooks to life. The brief ceremony closed with Kirkwood leading those assembled in prayer."

The press, always wanting to find an angle, reported that "the cemetery said that two dozen red carnations were ordered by a woman who declined to give her name." Of course everyone wondered, was it Ditra? There was no card on the delivered arrangement. As always, Rudy was not forgotten, by any means, as floral tributes poured in, including arrangements from E. and D. Baroni, the Rudolph Valentino Society of America in Buffalo, New York. And thus, the first year of a Ditra-less Valentino Memorial Service had drawn to an conclusion.

With Ditra being self-removed, the importance of Bud Testa in the organization of the annual memorial for Valentino vastly increased. It would prove to be a double edged sword. While Bud Testa was amazingly good at getting the press coverage that cemetery owner Jack Roth wanted, the future would prove that with few exceptions, Testa lacked imagination at keeping the services fresh and exciting. After the departure of Ditra Flame, the services began to have a rubber stamp like look to them. If you happened to miss any particular year, you needn't worry. The chances were that you could wait until the next year, and see the very same presentation, and more likely than not, the very same speakers. It didn't take long for the press as well as the attendees to realize that the void that Ditra left could not be easily filled. To his credit, it would appear that Bud didn't try.

Another individual who had spent many idle hours hovering at the crypt of Valentino over the recent years made a quick attempt to grab the reins of leadership of the Valentino faithful. He was one of Ditra's annoying detractors whom she had rightfully labeled as a "crackpot." His real name was Dominic Giordano, but to all the rest of the world he would be known as Rudolph Florentino. He was well known by the locals, as well as the police. He had turned his apartment located at 5546 ½ Hollywood Blvd. into a Valentino Shrine, complete with an Arab tent and imported desert sand. Scattered among his abode were piles of Valentino books, photos, and various memorabilia. Florentino, 52, attempted to fashion a resemblance to Rudy, even dressing as Valentino. Florentino, after much practice, also signed autographs in penmanship similar to Valentino's. Three years before, the police had been summoned to his apartment, as papers proclaimed in their headlines *Police Crash Valentino Shrine on Tip Off of Suicide Attempt*. Florentino, a brass welder by trade, laughed at the notion he would do himself in, saying "That's a farce," and that he had only been joking.

So, the day before the memorial services, the *Citizen News* on August 22, 1956 announced that Rudolph Florentino's apartment, aka The Valentino Shrine, would be open on August 23rd from 10 a.m. until that evening. The reporter specified that Florentino would lead the gathered fans to the Hollywood Memorial Park

Cemetery at noon to observe the annual memorial service for Valentino. After the services Florentino would again resume his hosting the faithful at his Valentino Shrine.

The memorial service for 1956 again, was brief. The speakers were the same. Silent star James Kirkwood gave tribute to Valentino saying "The spirit of romance Rudolph Valentino typified will live forever." Only thirty-five people attended the ceremony. Speaking on behalf of the Troupers Club, Kirkwood also recited the Lords Prayer, and mentioned that Valentino was "One of the most gracious persons I have ever known." Again, like clockwork, Belle Martell represented the Troupers and said at the conclusion that "He took the world by storm. He was romance and love to the thousands of women living drab and dull lives." At the conclusion of her remarks, Belle Martell raised her finger upward, smiled and said "Until next year!" Again, the press reported on the absence of the Lady In Black.

Interesting news was reported the following day, August 24, 1956. "Castellaneta, this south Italy town where Rudolph Valentino was born went all out yesterday to observe the 30th anniversary of the silent screen lover's death. There was a gala fiesta, prizes for the best window displays and a special Requiem Mass." This event marked a turning point of opinions in residents of Rudy's hometown. Unlike the hostile reception they gave Rudolph on his return visit in 1923, now, they seemed to embrace the legacy of Valentino.

James Kirkwood, left, and Belle Martell place a floral tribute at the Valentino
Memorial Service August 23, 1957

The Valentino Memorial Services would have an almost identical "cast" over the
next three years. With publicity man Bud Testa in charge, he seemed content to
let the service run on its own steam, which was in seemingly short supply. The
same speaker, silent actor James Kirkwood, would give the eulogy and was there
to represent the Masquers Club. While Mr. Kirkwood was always welcomed by the
crowd, through no fault of his own, he became predictable and redundant. The
ever reliable Mrs. Belle Martell would fare no better, when she would, again, step
forward to say a few sometimes ill chosen words in remembrance of Valentino.
When she spoke it was painfully evident to those in attendance that she didn't
know Valentino at all, and appeared to be along for the ride. But, like clockwork,

there she was, representing the Troupers Club. In fact, Belle even brought her husband into the act. He became the Trouper's official photographer. As the decade of the 1950's prepared to give way to the 1960's, there was still no Lady In Black, and the interest of the press seemed to dwindle. The memorial service write ups had shrunk from being prominent on the inside, front page, complete with photo, to a small, brief mention on the back pages, and usually without a picture to illustrate the story.

Rudolph Florentino dressed in sheik attire stands behind
spiritualist Carol McKinstry at a séance held at Falcon Lair
on the evening of August 23, 1951

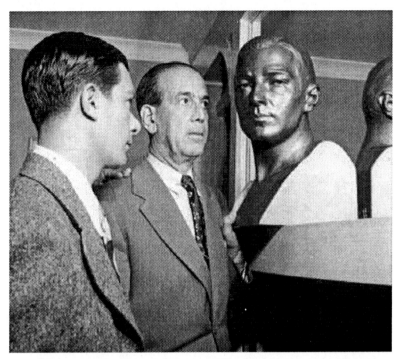

Alberto and Jean Valentino view a lifelike bust of their late relative

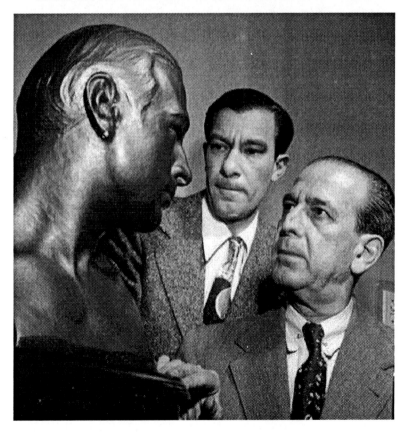

Jean Valentino poses next to a bust of his Uncle, Rudolph Valentino

1960 – 1969

This decade would witness the birth of the nostalgia craze, which in turn would give a big boost to the Valentino Memorial Services. Silent stars, those who were fortunate enough to still survive, would suddenly find themselves in demand for interviews, revered for their recollections, and nowhere was this more apparent than the newest television fad, the daytime talk shows. It wasn't uncommon to turn your television on to hear the tales of early cinema pioneers such as Mae Murray, Francis X. Bushman, Gloria Swanson and a host of others reminiscing on the silent era. Often their recollections turned to Rudolph Valentino. So, the year 1960 was optimistically anticipated by those who had attended the services for many years. The papers headline was direct. *Valentino Death Marked Simply.*

115

"Simply and quietly and with none of the pageantry of the past, the 34th anniversary memorial service for Rudolph Valentino was held. No women in black appeared among the 75 persons, who clustered in the narrow alcove leading to the modest crypt. There were a few of the faithful, like Helen Tull, who said she never has missed a Valentino Memorial Service." This year also marked the beginning of Bob Mitchell and his Boys Choir. However the paper noted that they did not come to sing but "to watch, stood solemn and wide eyed as Belle Martell told them 'Rudolph Valentino was a very great artist. We come here because we admired the artistry of this splendid performer.'" Again, James Kirkwood stepped forward to offer his usual eulogy. Another new addition to this years service pleased everyone. Roger Noble Burnham, a soft-spoken gentleman who had designed the Valentino Memorial statue *Aspiration* stepped forward to address the crowd. At 84 years old and in poor heath, Burnham had been forgotten by society, and was living on the hospitality of Valentino collector Mary Pfalzgraff in her huge home at 1041 West 21st Street, Los Angeles. On September 12, 1960, Mary Pfalzgraff wrote to Ditra Flame, who seemed confused as to who Roger was.

In her letter Mary explained that "I must clear up in your mind who Roger Burnham is, I have known him long before his statue of *Aspiration* was selected for the Valentino memorial to be placed in the park. He is a sweet and generous old gentleman, was 84 years old on August 11th and he lost his wife a year ago. So, we are taking care of him and have been appointed his guardian. He is beloved by everyone who knows him, has been in 'who's who' for over forty years. Was a teacher at Harvard University, father of the USC Trojans. Mr. Burnham had just completed a miniature figure of the *Aspiration* statue for me, and at the last minute I asked him if he'd like to go once, as he had never seen any Valentino Memorial Services, so I took him."

A new Lady In Black started appearing at the crypt. Ditra had been notified of this latest incarnation and on September 28, 1960 she wrote to Mary to say she had a suspicion about who it was. Ditra wrote "I have a strange feeling about the woman Jean Welles Vespia. I am wondering if she could be a plant of some kind by a studio, as I told you there are rumbles about a Lady In Black motion picture.

The studio would like to discredit me as the original Lady In Black, so they would have free sailing in writing a trumped up story. The only way to discredit me would be to have another Lady In Black, proving there is more than one. I'd like to know the 'inside' story." Ditra enclosed Jean Vespia's letter so Mary could read it for herself. Ditra went on to say "Read her letter, and be sure to return it, as I want it for my files. It might be important someday. Who knows. She has been going to the crypt three years, now she wants my permission (to dress as the Lady In Black). Nevertheless, she is on her own as far as I am concerned. Wouldn't I have felt silly had I gone to the crypt this year and found her there dressed as the Lady In Black? The newspapers would have really had a field day! You see, Mary, why I gave the whole thing up. I never had any way of knowing what kind of 'stunt' someone was going to pull, and put me in a bad light." Even though it had been six years since she had attended a Valentino Memorial Service, Ditra, through her correspondence (although behind the scenes) remained plugged into all the happenings on each anniversary.

Suddenly there was a new Lady In Black on the memorial forefront. She actually sought Ditra Flame's blessing, perhaps thinking that she wouldn't mind, since Ditra herself had given up the role. But the truth of the mater was Ditra had no intention whatsoever of giving her official blessings. It's interesting to note when that question was raised in a revealing television interview in 1961 with Paul Coates, she made it clear she would be glad for the tradition of the Lady in Black to continue after her death. However, since she was very much alive, she was in no hurry to pass the coveted torch of ultimate Hollywood mourning anytime soon.

Even if the torch wasn't passed, Ditra also couldn't let this opportunity slip away. Having a slight change of heart, she contacted Mrs. Vespia and implored her not to admit to anyone that she knew her, but to go ahead, appear, and see what would happen, but to be sure and to report back what transpired. It didn't take long to find out. Ditra wrote to Mary Pfalzgraff stating that "You should have seen how upset I was when I found out that Mrs. Tull had called the actress up and tried to put her off guard by being so sweet and inviting her over to see her collection. She told the actress she was so glad she came to the anniversary August 23rd and to come again and bring all her friends. Then she started pumping her about me. Was I going to be at the anniversary this next year. Then she got a barrage of phone calls giving her the third degree about me. All in all several men, and several women called her, one said he was a detective and had the goods on me that I paid her to appear at the crypt. But since you had been the only person who knew I had contacted this girl (actress) I began to wonder if you had unwittingly dropped the news. We shall see what happens next!"

On August 23, 1961 the memorial was acknowledging the 35th Anniversary of Valentino's passing. Again James Kirkwood delivered the eulogy stating that Valentino would be "Just as great" a movie star today, as he had been back in the silent era. "He had the personal magnetism that would make him great no matter what the era" Kirkwood told a convinced audience. This year, Bud Testa had a brilliant idea. He thought to invite the current Miss Spain who was on a goodwill tour of the United States, and her travel itinerary happened to place her in the vicinity of Hollywood on the day of the Valentino Memorial. Miss Carmen Cerverra, who had won her title in an international beauty contest, stepped forward to present an arrangement of red roses on behalf of all Valentino fans in Spain.

Statue of Rudolph Valentino dedicated in 1961 at his birthplace, Castellaneta, Italy

Anonymous Lady In Black is seen mourning alone at the Valentino crypt

Ditra poses on the mausoleum front steps on a visit to the Valentino crypt

Mary Pfalzgraff, sitting left, joins Ditra in bringing a long stemmed
rose to place at the Valentino crypt. Circa 1958

121

Long time regular Belle Martell had recently suffered health problems and was unable to attend. June Wood the assistant chaplain for the Troupers, filled in on her behalf, and would offer the opening and closing prayers. Cemetery officials were pleased to find in their head count, that the attendance numbers were beginning to climb once again. It was estimated that more than 100 people turned out for the Valentino service. Cables were received from Ditra's Valentino Memorial Guild, as well as Leslie Flint's London Memorial Guild.

Ironically, by 1962 Ditra became mild acquaintances with the Vespias, even visiting them at their home. However, the friendship didn't last long when Ditra visited and Jean told her that she and her mother had been getting sprit messages from Rudy every night. Ditra later wrote to Mary that "They got some while I was there, Rudy was supposed to have told me I was no good, and not helping him and to get out of his way, and forget him, etc., etc.! None of the 'messages' sounded at all like Rudy. I gave them to understand that I did not believe a word of it. I did not come to Hollywood to be told someone was getting spirit messages from Rudy." Seeking help, she enlisted Mary to assist. "If you have any idea what those people are up too, let me know, so I can protect myself!"

The 1962 memorial services got under way with some new faces. Jean Vespia was named in the press as a "strikingly handsome blonde artist," and gave her full name as Lucia Von Fravell Vespia, and she presented an oversized portrait of Valentino in his sheik attire. This was placed upright on the ledge of the stained glass window of the alcove where Valentino lay. Also participating at the services was Miss Stanny Von Baer of Holland who had been crowned Miss International of 1962. Perhaps Bud Testa assumed that the press interest in last year's Miss Spain attending the Valentino Memorial could be superseded in coverage by Miss International's attending. And he was indeed correct. Unlike Miss Spain in 1961, Miss International benefited from huge press coverage with her picture gazing upon the unique if not unusual portrait that Mrs. Vespia had brought.

Again, James Kirkwood as the papers noted had "read the memorial service for many years." Nobody knew that this year would sadly mark the end of James Kirkwood's tenure as the chief spokesperson at the Valentino Memorials. He would succumb on August 21, 1963. Through the years Kirkwood graciously stepped forward to offer his personal eulogies in remembrance of Valentino. His participation would be sorely missed, for not only had he been a silent film actor himself, offering first hand knowledge of the silent era, he had a much more personal connection. His third wife was Lila Lee, who had co-starred with Rudolph Valentino in the Paramount production of *Blood and Sand*. They had a son, James Kirkwood Jr. who was also in the industry, until his death in 1989.

Miss International 1962 attended the Valentino Memorial and places a bouquet by his crypt. Here she gazes at the unique painting on display

And so, another veteran of the silent era, one with a direct connection to the Valentino Memorial Services had fallen. At the 1963 services things livened up with the arrival of a new Lady In Black, this time hobbling on crutches. The press was there to catch the latest incarnation, and reported that "the mausoleum of Hollywood Memorial Park Cemetery was silent as onlookers watched the Lady In Black, heavily veiled and on crutches, slowly carry her wreath of a dozen red roses Friday to crypt 1205 where Valentino's body is interred. 'Sleep Well, Rudy' read the white ribbon on the wreath. The Lady In Black placed her wreath, stood facing the crypt for a moment, turned without speaking and made her way outside to a waiting black Cadillac limousine" which had Arizona license plates. "Although she appeared to be in her 60's the black veil disguised her features."

Unidentified Lady in Black arrives on crutches with her flowers for the Valentino
Memorial Service on August 23, 1963

The *Herald Examiner* reported that "a mysterious woman in black showed up today to commemorate the 37th anniversary of the death of Rudolph Valentino. Only this time she really was a mystery because not even a public relations spokesman for the Valentino event, one Bud Testa, knew the woman. 'I never saw her before in my life' Testa said. Continuing, "Testa said the original Lady In Black was Ditra Flame, 'and that is not Ditra' he said, pointing to this years star attraction. The woman was escorted by a white haired portly gentleman. Neither would talk or give their names."

With the departure of Ditra ten years before, and now with the death of James Kirkwood, and the removal of Belle Martell due to illness, the 1964 Valentino Memorial Service was in major need of a face lift. The usual crackpot characters plagued each service, including Rudolph Florentino, Mary Hammin, and of course the Swiss spiritualist, Amanda. More times than not, they were simply ignored by those in charge of the program. This year's memorial was led by June Woods who had stepped in to fill the void left by Belle Martell in representing the Hollywood Troupers. Over a hundred and fifty people were in attendance at the brief, quiet service.

The new crop of fake Ladies In Black, popping up every so often, was not lost on Ditra Flame. From her correspondence it's painfully evident that it bothered her, however what could she do? By her own choice she had left the field wide open to any person to don a black dress and veil and grab the spotlight for herself. She felt that her legacy was being cheapened. She had written in her scrapbook next to the newspaper photograph of the Lady In Black on crutches, "Personally I believe this stunt was done on purpose to ridicule me." Her only options would be to either ignore them or to return. She reached out to long time friends Lita and Tommy McIntire, whom she had known since 1927.

On August 10, 1965 Ditra wrote them, thanking them for sending photos of their grandchildren to her. She said "I want to thank you for the lovely pictures.

I'd like to see them sometime. And of course I'd love to see you, dear people of my girlhood. My how time flies! I can't believe we are really getting along in years." Then Ditra dropped the bombshell. "I would like to go to Valentino's anniversary this year. But I hate to go alone as I usually have someone with me. No one to go with me this year. I don't know why I want to go this time, maybe the world is coming to an end – or me – who knows?" And so, it was set. After an eleven year absence Ditra would return, not garbed as the Lady In Black, but rather in a yellow flowered dress.

She wouldn't be the only one returning. This year saw the return of another original, when George Ullman decided he would like to see how the service had evolved over the years. With both Ullman and Flame there, it was like a reunion of the old cast. Not dating as far back, but still considered an old timer, Belle Martell returned. Recovering from a stroke, she returned for the 1965 memorial service, confined to a wheelchair. She was warmly and tearfully welcomed back by the faithful who had been attending the services long enough to remember her.

Silent actor Richard Arlen delivered a soft-spoken eulogy to Valentino. As usual, the fly in the ointment was the Swiss spiritualist, Amanda Tannarose who arrived this year wearing a bizarre headdress and was generally disruptive. After the services, Ditra wrote to George Ullman to inquire about the identity of a man she had seen at the memorial services. She suspected it was Russell Birdwell, the publicity man who had long ago laid claim to having hired the original Lady In Black to appear at the *Aspiration* statue. Always trying to prove that she was not the creation of a publicity gimmick, Ditra sought to find out if the person she saw was Birdwell. On September 14, 1965 she asked Ullman "Wasn't Russell Birdwell the tall, rather impressive gray haired man interviewing several people at the crypt this year? Did you see him?" Ditra went on to joke about Amanda saying "I hope Amanda, the one who met Rudy on the celestial planes takes off for Venus in a flying saucer by next years services!" In a letter dated September 17, 1965 George Ullman wrote back and told her "That man was not Birdwell. He was some kind of a nut who told me that he represented some news services but couldn't remember the names when I asked him!" And, to add his own touch of humor to match Ditra's, he wrote "Isn't Amanda the name of a freezer?"

June Wood, left joins Bell Martell, center, placing a floral tribute at the
Valentino crypt. Swiss spiritualist Amanda Tannarose is seen gazing at
Valentino's grave marker. Circa August 23, 1965

So, the return of both Ullman and Flame to the Valentino Memorial after an absence of many years only proved that although many of the originals were no longer around, for those who were, the Valentino Memorial still held interest. To cover her bases, on the same day as she wrote to George Ullman, she wrote to Bud Testa. She asked him the same questions, but went into more detail about why she felt it was Birdwell. Ditra wrote to Bud saying "Everyone was so rushed August 23rd I did not have a chance to ask you a question that you may be able to answer and here it is. Wasn't Russell Birdwell at the anniversary services August 23rd? Though I have never in years past met him and never saw him at the services before, I have seen pictures of him and I am almost certain he was the tall, rather impressive gray haired man who asked me several questions and then he asked me what I thought about Birdwell claiming he invented the Lady In Black. At that moment I had a hunch I was talking to the man himself. I told him that Mr. Birdwell certainly didn't invent me as I have been going to Valentino's crypt since 1926 and I had two people with me to prove it. Now, I can't imagine why Birdwell and his inkwell are so bent on claiming he invented the Lady In Black, unless it is to hold on to the rights in case a picture is ever made of same. But that is flimsy because you can't copyright a title. I wish he would put his swords away. Of course I know he wrote a lot on Marion Benda, the one who committed suicide, so that places him in another camp. I still haven't gotten over the article in *Hush-Hush* magazine, March 1956 titled *The Press Agents Trick that Fooled the World For 30 Years.* In this article the writer said 'Ditra Flame said that she had been paid by a press agent to put on her act each year.' Of course I never said such a thing because I never had a press agent in my life. I cannot understand how writers can get away with putting words in the mouth of living people and get away with it." Ditra closed her letter to Testa saying "I was rather surprised there were not more people at the crypt this year. And where was the press? All TV news. Channel 7 was very good. We, the Rudolph Valentino Guild used to get four column spreads, pictures and all. This year nothing about the Valentino services in the papers. All I have ever wanted was to keep Rudy's name alive. I guess it is time to change the script."

The press returned to cover the 40th anniversary in 1966. Also returning was Alberto Valentino, along with his son Jean as well as Jean's wife, Maria, and their daughter Sylvia. For yet another year, Ditra Flame returned, wearing a baby blue colored dress. She carried with her a single red rose which she later placed at Valentino's crypt. Again for the sake of the reporters Ditra repeated her story as to why she had stopped attending as the Lady In Black. She was quick to let them know that she still considered herself the original. "I'm the original Lady In Black, whether anyone likes it or not." Papers reported how the crowd was slimming down in size when they said "it appeared during the 40th such ceremony, that things may be taming down a bit for the memory of the great sheik. Only 75 persons attended, and a good portion of them were newsmen, publicists and tourists, rather than the bona fide bereaved. Few cried, and if anyone fainted, it was probably more from heat and lack of air, than emotion." The memorial was conducted by June Woods who said Valentino was "A man who had the love of every woman and the respect of every man." While Ditra received ample coverage by attending, it is amazing that not one single reporter saw fit to inquire what the Valentino family thought about the continuance of these services.

1967 would see the release of the much anticipated *Valentino* biography by Irving Shulman. Shulman's tome would quickly rise to the top, as the most revealing, in-depth, informative, not to mention the heaviest researched book ever done on Rudolph Valentino to that time. It would be surpassed four decades later with the 2003 release of *Dark Lover* by Emily Leider.

At the Valentino Memorial Services the cast was pretty much the same. The ever-welcome Belle Martell was there along with new spokeswoman June Wood. Again, the services had hit a lull. Ditra did not attend, but her profound words lived on. "It's time to change the script." As dusk set on the turbulent decade of the 1960's the Valentino Memorial trudged along, proceeding by rote. The original attendees were thinning out with each passing year. The 1970's would bring forth the birth of a major nostalgia boom and this would, in effect inject renewed life into the Valentino Memorial Service.

Ditra would not allow the closure of the decade without having her say. In her letter to Tommy and Lita McIntire she minced no words on what she thought of Shulman's tell all. On February 24, 1968 she was quick to gloat about her unique chance. She spelled it all out, in a most revealing letter, saying that "I had the experience of a lifetime, Thursday morning at 1:00 a.m. I couldn't sleep so I turned on my radio and just happened to get KFI. I heard the broadcaster say 'This is KFI and my guest is Irving Shulman, the author of the book *Valentino*.' My ears went up and I heard him say, 'Tell me Mr. Shulman, about the Lady In Black'. Shulman went into a long song and dance about the story being concocted by Russell Birdwell, a reporter, and then he went into a long talk about Ditra Flame. That did it. I dashed to the phone and called KFI. The operator at KFI said hang on, I'll get you in to talk to Mr. Shulman. They canceled all calls and held me on the line because I told them who I was. While I was waiting to get on the line, I heard Belle Martell come on the air, and of all the things she said about me! She ran me down at the heels and said the Valentino family was on her side against me and so on ad infinitum. I bet she was shocked to hear my voice come on the air right after her and that was a lucky break for me.

Well, I had a real good confab with Shulman and believe me I put him straight about what he said about me in his book. The conversation became so interesting I was kept on the air for a half-hour (at my expense of course) however, I got over to the public my side of the thing and I would do it again no matter what it cost. There was one interesting thing Shulman said. I told him that all the stories written about me had been fabricated, and a pack of lies, except *Photoplay* magazine. I said that everyone has made money on me for years writing their trash. He said, 'why on earth didn't you sue?' I said 'that takes money, and I didn't want to drag the Valentino name through any more mud.' He said 'don't you know that you have done yourself more harm than good by not suing.' Ditra concluded her letter saying that "Shulman told me I had better write a book and tell the truth about myself. So, I am busy trying to get the story together. I should leave something behind in my own words."

While it is doubtful at the early hour of 1:00 a.m., that she had much of an audience, to Ditra, it was the principal. She had gone one-on-one with Irving Shulman and had walked away vindicated. To her, that was what mattered. In fact her interview went so well that Shulman had his agent approach Ditra to inquire about the possibility of her making a joint television appearance with him, in his promotion tour for his *Valentino* book. Defending herself on the radio show was one thing, but to promote his book was quite another. On March 4, 1968 she dashed off a rejection letter to Steve Adler who was Shulman's publicity agent, working at Promotion In Motion at 6515 Sunset Blvd. Ditra replied "Your notation of February 29th received requesting me to appear with Mr. Shulman on a KNXT TV show. I think such a show would be interesting and advantageous to KNXT and also to Mr. Shulman in the way of more publicity for his *Valentino* book.

However I cannot see where I would be enhancing my life's work in Christian service." Ditra continued with why she was giving this a thumbs down. "I am not interested in my press image as the Lady In Black nor aiding Mr. Shulman's promotion of his book since he never took the trouble to interview me before writing about me. Since he preferred to place me in his land of cuckoos, in his book, it would be foolish for me to appear with him on TV. I take issue with Mr. Shulman mainly because in his book he questioned the sincerity of my conversion. Right after he said that I joined the Rose of Sharon Evangelical Ministry and years later I appeared at the Valentino crypt and spoke to fifty teenagers and beseeched them to worship Valentino. I have many witnesses to the fact that this never happened, including Mr. George Ullman who was there. Mr. Shulman should have sense enough to know that no Christian ever beseeched anyone to worship anyone, save Jesus Christ. Personally, I believe he knows this, but to serve his own purpose, he placed me in an insincere light. If such are his methods, nothing would be gained by my appearance with him. For this reason, I must refuse your offer to appear with Mr. Shulman."

While Ditra was declining any part in helping to promote the Shulman book, she was quick to write to George Ullman to see how the book set with him. The last time they had seen each other was at the 1965 memorial. In her letter Ditra joked with Ullman, saying "Here we go again! Have you read the new *Valentino* by Irving Shulman?" After complaining about her treatment, and having been placed in the 'Cuckooland' chapter, she tips the scale back to Ullman, saying "He didn't treat you very kindly either." At that memorial Ditra said "I did not open my mouth to anyone but Richard Arlen" (he gave the eulogy) "I thanked him for his kindness. He was later told off by the leaders because he spoke kindly of me." Offering a sympathetic word, she touched on Ullman's ongoing legal battles with the Valentino family. Ditra told Ullman "I know you have had your ups and downs with the Valentino name—too bad. It seems all they can do is sue somebody. Guess they got a good settlement on the Dexter picture. Wonder if they have sued Chaw Mank on his *Intimate and Shocking Expose* of Valentino? They called Rudy a pansy and everything else. Wonder what the Valentino's think of that? I also wonder what they will do when they read about Rudy's arrest in the Shulman book. I never could find out what he was picked up for, if he was, so what. Look at the kids nowadays, they *like* it in jail." Then Ditra plunged in with her question "Of course there have been so many stories about that, I wish I knew the truth about it. Did Rudy ever tell you? He should have so you could have protected his name. Wonder what the Valentino's think about that! They are so snooty. Sorry, I should not sound like a cat, but I really have no tender feelings for them." And then Ditra closed her long letter with "I just wanted you to know that I am not cuckoo as they make me out to be and I don't think they are fair to you either. I don't think you are as 'crooked' as they make you out to be. What a world! Glad we don't have to put up with it forever."

1970 – 1979

The era of nostalgia began to bud in the late 1960's but really bloomed by the 1970's. The Valentino Memorial Services benefited, in part because people had a new-found sense of respect for the past. With that respect came renewed awe for the first time appearance of silent screen star, Mary MacLaren. Mary was a very soft spoken, sweet lady. Her Valentino connection was undeniable. Her dressing room at Universal Studios was next to Rudolph Valentino's. "Rudy used to come into my dressing room every morning and kiss me. The white haired, slender woman smiles through a haze of cigarette smoke in the marbled lobby of the Hollywood Memorial Park Cemetery. 'I have to start the day out right,' he would say. I was only 15 years old, when I met Valentino, you know. But we were very, very close friends."

"In a marble room, high walls lined with bronze plaqued crypts, the faithful have flocked to pay their respects. They crowd a room where soft light filters in through a stained glass window, and they strain to see the speakers. A short, fat woman booms out the 23rd Psalm, and bowed heads echo it back. Another woman, carrying a tiny dog in her purse, stands on tiptoes to glimpse the ceremony. Byron Palmer delivers a eulogy as television crews pack up and leave the room." Another man, Aleck Novaro, gave an interview saying "I tried out as an extra for *The Sheik*, but Valentino said I was too young." The head of the Valentino Guild of London, Leslie Flint, was present, and stated "He wasn't just a movie star. Too many people are silly and just come for the sensationalist. But I stood in the back, ya' know, 'cause I didn't want the publicity. I think some respect should be paid to his memory." Bud Testa was quoted as saying he had been organizing the memorial services for the past 15 years. He told the reporter that Ditra Flame was the original Lady In Black and her last appearance had been four years ago.

The following year, the Valentino Memorial might well have qualified for placement in Shulman's 'Cuckooland' chapter. For the 45th anniversary, it was reported that a "Miss Eddie Crispell played the part of the mod Lady In Black. She wore a see-through black blouse and wet look hot pants with knee high black vinyl boots, all topped off with a long Spanish style black veil. 'I am symbolic of the lost love and romance Hollywood has experienced. I'm not dressed this way to mock the old ways, but rather to bring the past to the present.'"

Eddie Crispell joined publicist Christopher Harris, attending the Valentino Memorial for a high profile protest over the demise of the golden age of Hollywood. Without offering specifics, he offered only "I am here to represent what we have lost in Hollywood. We want to build a shrine in memory of Valentino." His bizarre appearance further undermined his credibility. He was "dressed in a 1920's tuxedo, and had white grease paint on his face, giving the tall thin publicity man a definite Dracula-like air." Harris went on to state "I'm wearing makeup in protest for what has happened in the past 45 years here. I represent the Foundation of the Memory of Rudolph Valentino." Repeating himself, he said "We're here to protest. We want to get Valentino a better place to rest. He's not happy here, he belongs in his native village in Italy."

He further mentioned how only days before the 45th anniversary, he had contacted Paramount Studios, situated adjacent to the cemetery. "I called Paramount, and asked them to send a dozen roses. They asked me if he ever worked for them, and when I told them he did, they said they didn't have the petty cash." As they were setting up, while Christopher Harris was addressing the press, members of the Troupers Club arrived with large wreaths of flowers. As the memorial started, Elinor Klein, the new Chaplain of the Trouper's Club, and June Woods successor, "was introduced and led a reading of the 23rd Psalm." Spotting the use of a Jewish Bible, a bystander asked "What kind of service is this going to be?" "I thought he was Catholic."

"Mrs. Klein pushed forward with the program and introduced silent screen star Mary MacLaren who declared 'I hope I can speak without becoming too emotional. I knew him' and then was overcome with tears." Mary then composed herself and introduced Hal Dawson, who also paid tribute to the lasting legacy of Rudolph Valentino. As Dawson was speaking of Valentino's passing in 1926, activist Crispell Harris "whispered loudly" that he was murdered. One of the members of the Troupers verbalized, just as loudly, "Let us finish." With an agenda, Harris followed up in a loud voice heard by all who attended that "We're here to protest." Mrs. Klein made an attempt to have someone introduce her again, in order to give a closing prayer on behalf of Valentino. This was the first time the services had been hijacked for cheap publicity of an activist group. Their motives may have been sincere, but they had overplayed their hand, and it was apparent that they were not warmly received. No further trace of the so-called 'Foundation for the Preservation of the Memory of Rudolph Valentino' ever again materialized.

As the Valentino Memorial was rolled out for another year in 1972, the 'script' as Ditra had mentioned, hadn't been changed. Once again the ever-wry Mrs. Elinor Klein was there to lead the services. Spotting the newspaper reporters who hungered to get a snapshot, she struck a pose and jokingly told them "Take the picture, honey, double chins and all." The paper called the Troupers organization "an aging actor's club" and noted the unique makeup of Elinor Klein. She had "a black satin dress that reached to the ground, blue eyeliner with two blue dots under each eye."

Once again, Mary MacLaren spoke, saying of Rudy, "He was the sweetest person I've ever known, but the best thing about him was his love of animals." Mary, caught up in the moment, pushed the thought a bit further and told the hushed audience that "I believe in reincarnation and it is my hope that this man (Valentino) will return to save the animals. They need it." A voice from the audience called out "Amen" and Mary MacLaren began to cry, as she made her way back to her seat.

Next up was 1920's crooner Rudy Vallee who gave the eulogy and made mention of Rudolph Valentino's "Physical appeal to five million women." When Vallee finished his remarks, Mrs. Klein returned to the podium to conclude the service by reading the 23rd Psalm. As the crowd began to leave she boldly barked "Every Sunday night for $1.25 you can see a new show at the Trouper's Club. Older actors giving their all. See a lot of stars, come this week." With this tacky sales pitch, it was painful to the genuine and sincere, that once again the Valentino Memorial Service was going through a painful transition.

The focus seemed to be on everything *but* Rudolph Valentino. Second-rate talent, publicity seekers, fringe showbiz characters, guaranteed crackpots and faux mourners had infiltrated the once solemn service, to push their cause or organization into the limelight. Very few people behind the podium seemed to have any great love, knowledge or even respect towards the memory of Rudolph Valentino. The service limped along the next couple of years with no real guiding force. Perhaps Bud Testa ran out of ingenious ways to make the service sparkle again. He was aware that most of the people who knew Rudy had already passed away. Then he thought back to 1951 when Columbia had sent Anthony Dexter over to the services and had gotten free publicity for their *Valentino* motion picture. He knew that was a sure-fire method to spice up the services. At the same time, Testa was aware that ABC was producing a television movie of the week based on Valentino. For the 1975 Valentino Memorial, it was arranged for the star Franco Nero to appear at the service, and to give the eulogy about the man he would portray on television. The idea had worked before, so why not now? Once again the Valentino Memorial was thrust back onto the front pages. Nero was accompanied by Suzanne Pleshette, who portrayed June Mathis in the film. They sat together until Testa introduced him, to the delight of the audience. Once again, it would be current Valentino projects that brought a renewed vigor to the memorial services.

A month later, S. George Ullman died at the age of 89. He was never financially able to get out from under the pile of lawsuits the Valentino family had levied against him. Ullman had made arrangements with UCLA Medical School that upon his death to have his body donated for research. Thus, another important, direct Valentino connection passed quietly from the scene.

The year 1976 saw a yearlong patriotic celebration saluting the Bi-Centennial of the United States. This same year would mark the golden anniversary for those who had remained steadfast and faithful for half a century, to the memory of Rudolph Valentino. Not since the early years had there been such a turnout. An estimated one thousand people jammed into the Cathedral Mausoleum on August 23rd 1976 to witness the outpouring of affection at this milestone Valentino Memorial Service.

After opening prayers, actor Jon Hall (*Hurricane*) stepped forward to give a brief eulogy telling the attendees that Valentino had inspired him in his quest to become an actor. He also said that perhaps Valentino's "romantic spirit may also have inspired the population explosion in the years that followed his death." In attendance were two people who had been film stars. Mary MacLaren made her eighth consecutive appearance, and told reporters and fans alike, her now familiar story that while working at Universal someone had asked her if she had seen the handsome new actor in the dressing room next to hers. She said she had not, but went over to meet him. Ready, willing, and able, Mary found herself thrust in the spotlight each year at the Valentino Memorial Service. She was surrounded by well wishers and people who yearned to hear firsthand accounts of Valentino from someone who had actually known him.

Another actress drawing less of a crowd but who was noticed by the press, was "one time cinema queen Corinne Calvet" who was spotted in the alcove where Valentino's crypt is, burning "pungent sticks of incense and philosophized quietly about how Valentino provided 'a channel for the energy of love.'" Another person attending was the self-professed astrologer to the stars, Anthony Norvell. He was on the program of guest speakers, and he spoke of how he had met Valentino when he was 18 and he had prepared a horoscope for Valentino. He revealed that the personal horoscope prophesied that Valentino would become a great lover but would pay a dear price, by dying young.

Not all those attending the 50th anniversary of the Valentino Memorial were reverent. Two men appeared dressed in sheik attire. One, was an Egyptian man who identified himself only as Bob. The second sheik gave his name as "The Owl" and within a short time was busy handing out flyers to a stage show called "Hollywood Hoot." And to finalize the day's activities a mysterious Lady In Black, in a black dress and heavy black veil, showed up, assisted by a burly older gentleman, and slowly made her way down the marble corridors as she leaned heavily on her cane. "She knelt in front of Valentino's crypt, blew a kiss at the cold marble, then departed as mysteriously as she had come." Once again, a Lady In Black whose identity was known but to God, had, through her appearance, added to the continuing of the legend.

The heavy press coverage of the Valentino Memorial Service was not lost on the Hollywood film industry. While taking a loftier approach, the Screen Actor's Guild (SAG) hosted a reception followed by a screening of *The Four Horseman* at the Academy Theater on the evening of August 23rd. One very impressed attendee was

Tony Altamirano. He who wrote on August 25, 1976 that "I saw Jean and Alberto Valentino, and Alberto introduced me to his granddaughter, Jean's girl. A display of personal Valentino family things included telegrams at the time of his death, canceled bank checks, several gold plaques, the large gold bust of Rudolph Valentino was beautiful!" *Daily Variety*, reporting on the event said that "to counter the annual display of crackpot homage to Rudolph Valentino, Hollywood celebs decided it was high time this year to pay serious tribute to the actor." Clearly they aimed the "crackpot" snipe at the goings on at the Valentino Memorial Service at Hollywood Memorial Park Cemetery. They concluded that the "Screen Actors Guild celebration cut many notches above the usual goings on at Hollywood Mausoleum."

And so, half a century after his death, Rudolph Valentino was well remembered. In all the hub-bub of pseudo Sheiks at the crypt, the appearance of yet another mysterious Lady In Black, (mourning for a record-breaking fifty years), bizarre incense burning at his crypt by another actress, nowhere did reporters ponder, in print what he himself may have thought about of all this.

A year later, Mary MacLaren once again was on hand. She had fine-tuned her association with Valentino to include new insights. She told reporters at the 1977 Valentino Memorial what she recalled when she heard that Valentino had fallen ill. Mary told attendees, "I was walking through a hotel lobby in London. I heard that Valentino was gravely ill. I walked to the park across the street and cried. I knew that he was going to die." Transporting herself to current times, Mary revealed "I dreamed about Valentino last night." She felt confident that "If my mother hadn't interfered, I could have become the first Mrs. Valentino."

The memorial lineup included television personality Virginia Graham who confessed that while she had never met Rudolph Valentino, she wanted to pay tribute by participating. She went on to explain that she thought Valentino "Released a quality of kindness." The Pomona California paper *Progress Bulletin* eyed a person who was on the verge of becoming a major player in the upcoming Valentino Memorial Services. They solicited a quote from Estrellita Del Regil. She told them "I come every year because there is something that attracts me here. He was the most beautiful, handsome man in the world. No one today has this attraction. His veins were full of mysteries. I often come here and pray to him."

As the future would eventually prove, Del Regil would soon become ingrained within the structure of the Valentino Memorial, and could easily qualify as one of the most colorful characters in the entire history of the services. But for now, she kept her story to a minimum. The spotlight this year was on someone with credentials without question. For the first time since 1953 Ditra Flame reappeared in full Lady In Back regalia. Stating her case that "I was very heartbroken over hearing of Elvis Presley's death, when I saw pictures of the crowd weeping at the gates in Memphis, I thought maybe now this generation understands how us older people felt about Valentino." Another unidentified woman also thought of the Presley connection. She exclaimed "There were thousands here last year. I guess with the Presley thing this was kind of anti-climatic." She vowed that no matter what, "Valentino will always be with us."

Returning guest Anthony Norvell spoke again. He told the throng that "Every so often there flashes on the horizon of earth, a great star who becomes forever enshrined in the memory of man. Such a star was Valentino, who had a brief life span of only a few years, but who is enshrined forever in the hearts and minds of all people." Everyone nodded in agreement, and then, with the final closing prayer of the 23rd Psalm, another year concluded.

A final hurrah for a grand lady. Ditra Flame gladly signs an autograph for Michael Back, (back to camera) at the Valentino Memorial Service on August 23, 1977.

Television personality Virginia Graham is the keynote speaker at the Valentino Memorial Service in 1977

The Valentino Memorial Services were quite tame in 1978. Once more Mary MacLaren told her heartfelt, yet familiar reminisces of Valentino. Even the press began to pick up on this by saying "she carried in her hand a large magnifying glass to help her read her notes." Yet they acknowledged after all these years that it was "a message she mostly knew by heart." Once at the podium Mary mentioned that she never had the opportunity to appear in a film with Valentino, but told the audience "My beautiful sister, Katherine MacDonald made two movies with him. One was called 'Passion's Playground', the other one I don't remember." She concluded her remarks by chuckling, "I never went to see either one."

Silent star Mary MacLaren graces the cover of the April 1921 edition of Photoplay

Mary MacLaren as she looked in her movie star days

Mary MacLaren is assisted to the Valentino grave by unnamed friends, to place her floral offering at the conclusion of the Valentino Memorial Service 1978

Silent star Mary MacLaren tells her familiar story at the Valentino Memorial Services for 1978 MacLaren spoke for 17 consecutive years

Next on the program, an 'aura analyst' Barbara Martin, came fully equipped, and "displayed her talk with a poster board diagram showing Valentino's health lines and thought forms." Valentino's "silhouette was in poster board gold, surrounded by painted on clouds of soft muted colors." Miss Martin explained to the audience how she had come to obtain this information, and said "I was absolutely amazed when I stood by his crypt to get inside that deep soul level. I could feel this absolute expansive flow of his love." She droned on, perhaps oblivious of Valentino's personal abhorrence to being associated with the word pink (powder puff), and finished her presentation by saying "Valentino had magnificent pinks and rose reds that just flowed out from his heart center. And he had silvery hues of power. He had this tremendous magnetic aura." The people attending had no clue what all the colors meant, yet they remained polite.

Bud Testa then introduced the surviving half of the successful vaudeville singing team of The Duncan Sisters. Vivian Duncan provided a nostalgic musical interlude by singing a tune she herself had composed in honor of Rudolph Valentino. She even accompanied herself, playing her ukulele, the conclusion of her song "When we go, you and I, to join those Saints in the sky, where roses neither fade or die - oh yes, we'll see Valentino there."

The service this year was intermittently amusing albeit mostly repetitive. The one thing that stood out, was the emergence from anonymity of Estrellita Del Regil. A year before she had casually mentioned that there was something that drew her to the Valentino Memorial Service and that she often came to pray at his crypt. Now, with Ditra Flame again out of the picture, Estrellita stepped forward with a newly concocted story. Dressed for the role, she was "wearing a black floor length evening gown, with elbow length black gloves, a black straw hat, and a long flowing black scarf. She carried white rosary beads." She told the reporters who were either new to the scene or didn't care as long as they got their story, that "My mother knew him. She was a dancer in New York. Valentino came to our house a few times, but I never met him."

First-rate Vaudeville performer Vivian Duncan plays her ukulele as she sings a self composed song dedicated to Rudolph Valentino at the 1978 Valentino Memorial Services

Estrellita, who would come to find unique ways each year of decorating the alcove where Valentino's body rests, had this year "placed a plastic pot of white daisies on a white marble shelf next to Valentino's crypt. Then she posed for photographers." A green ribbon extended from the plastic pot of flowers, and she had written "In loving remembrance. Adieu, Adieu, Adieu."

The first performance of her Lady In Black role didn't play well with the entire audience. Seeing her and another new lady dressed in ebony, one person was quoted as muttering that "They're impostors." Not caring about the unreceptive crowd, Estrellita was determined to continue her quest to seize the Lady In Black title.

The Valentino Memorial Services hadn't seen the last of Estrellita Del Regil. A footnote to the 1978 services was that two weeks prior, Jean Acker, Rudolph

Valentino's first wife had died at the age of 85. She had been the only wife of Rudolph Valentino to ever come to pay respects on August 23rd. Although her name was not mentioned during the 52nd memorial services, she would take his name to her grave. Buried at Holy Cross Cemetery her brass name plaque reads Jean Acker Valentino.

Mary MacLaren, left, Reverend Pilson Potter, center, and keynote speaker, George Jessel, right sit together for the Valentino Memorial Service August 23, 1979

In 1979 the eulogy at the 53rd Valentino Memorial Service would be offered by renowned Toastmaster General of the United States, George Jessel. He "delivered a five minute eulogy, noting no less than four times how Valentino 'made the hearts of millions of women flutter without ever uttering a word.' Jessel later clarified his remarks for a group of reporters. 'Oh, Valentino' Jessel said. 'I knew him when he was a gigolo making old ladies happy in New York. What a guy.'" It was apparent to everyone who attended that Jessel didn't know Valentino at all, nor had he even bothered to prepare for his remarks, preferring instead to speak off the cuff. Aside from that, the brief 45 minutes the service lasted also included, once again, Mary MacLaren, and a calypso tribute to Valentino performed by a

148

singer named Sir Lancelot. Aura analyst Barbara Martin repeated her previous years color charts to what the newspapers reported was "the bewildered crowd." Also pushing her way forward in the alcove where Rudolph lay, was a lady that was identified as the German contingent of the Valentino Fan Club. Miss Ulrike Doniger was dressed all in black. "There are at least 300 members in Berlin," she remarked. As she continued, in a somewhat suspicious German accent, she continued "I have come to represent Germany at these services for this great Italian – he was Italian wasn't he? – actor."

Also true to her promise to return, Estrellita Del Regil settled in for an encore performance. Each year she attended she seemed to embellish her story, building on it year by year. Now she proclaimed that not only did her mother know Rodolpho from his early days in New York, but that Estrellita herself had visited Valentino's crypt on every August 23rd for "At least the past 20 years." Most old timers just shook their head in amazement. Possibly in an effort to prove her over-all devotion, on the marble wall adjacent to Valentino's crypt, Estrellita "taped up a photograph of herself, kneeling – flowers in one hand, Rosary beads in the other, on Valentino's Hollywood Boulevard star" on the Walk of Fame. In the alcove where Rudy lay, with people swirling about after the ceremonies had concluded, she was seen by the crypt muttering to no one in particular over and over "I believe, I believe." And so, yet another decade of the Valentino Memorial Services had drawn to a uneven closure.

Estrellita Del Regil's mother whom Estrellita claimed to be the original
Lady In Black. When she died she was buried at Forest Lawn cemetery but in
1989 Estrellita had her moved to Hollywood Memorial Cemetery

Estrellita Del Regil models a most unique dress, circa 1933. A photo of Rudolph
Valentino can be seen in her midriff section

1980-1989

The Valentino Memorial entered a brand new decade, with a sprinkling of old faces still on the scene. From the Troupers came Reverend Pilson Potter who once more opened the 1980 memorial with a prayer. Like clockwork, Mary MacLaren stepped forward to repeat her oft told story of her personal association with Valentino. The gathered crowd listened as a new speaker, Daniel Williams delved into the so-called reincarnation of Valentino. Miss MacLaren listened eagerly too, as she had been approached several times over the previous years, at the Valentino Memorial by young men who had professed to be the reincarnation of Rudy. Always polite, Mary listened, but never saw fit to give her blessing, or to endorse any of them. Not one had ever convinced her that they were the real deal. Even at her advanced age, Mary MacLaren knew there could only be but one Rudolph Valentino.

Bud Testa then introduced Tawni Sims who was the founder of the Las Vegas Valentino Club. The music chosen this year was a new song by Paloma Carrillo Woods entitled *Memories of Valentino*. One verse said "Then he was gone, many tears were shed. By loving hearts that bled – Now cheer that his memories are with us here, and his spirit every year seems to be with us too."

In keeping with Bud Testa's idea of having a member from the motion picture industry speak the eulogy, this year he invited respected veteran film actor and television star Lew Ayres. He spoke about what an inspiration Valentino was to the Hollywood community.

The anniversary date in 1981 fell on a Sunday. When that happened, it was traditional to hold the service the following day. Accordingly, the 55th Valentino Memorial was held on Monday August 24, 1981. More than one hundred people showed up to hear a brief eulogy offered once more by legendary showman and singer, Rudy Vallee. He "remembered Valentino as a magnetically attractive man whose public appearances caused furors. Vallee named the late George Raft as the one man he had met, who came closest to having Valentino's charm and personality." Rounding out the service was Mary MacLaren, who told the crowd that "she felt that Valentino's spirit was present at the services," Ivar Novello, a cousin of actor Ivor Novello, read a poem dedicated to Valentino. Troupers Chaplain Reverend Pilson Potter concluded the services by reading the 23rd Psalm from the Holy Bible.

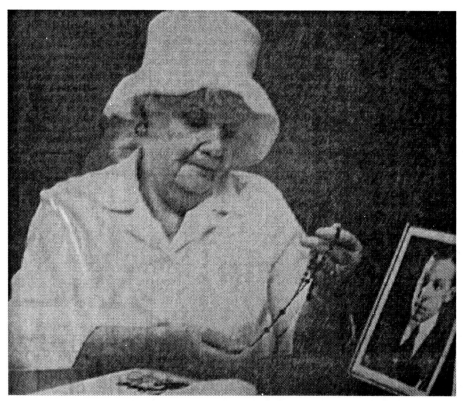

Ditra Flame looks over some of the items in her Valentino collection. Citing poor health and eyesight Flame sought a ride to the 1981 Valentino Memorial Services but did not end up attending

In a sidebar story to the 1981 service, The *Daily Report* newspaper blared a headline "Lady In Black – old friend of Valentino needs ride to graveside to keep vigil." Warning that "the legendary Lady In Black may not be able to make her famous rendezvous at the crypt," the article stated that due to ill health, and poor eyesight Ditra Flame couldn't make the drive from her home in Ontario. Interviewed three days before the event, Ditra said "I'm still going to try and make it." Sadly, Ditra didn't find her ride, and unfortunately she would be forced to miss the 1981 Valentino Memorial Service.

Estrellita Del Regil worked her way into the newspapers yet again, for the 1982 memorial services. Once more she dressed as the Lady In Black and wandered aimlessly up and down the halls. The services this year would be extremely brief with only three guests lined up to speak. Once again the services were opened in prayer by Pilson Potter, then Mary MacLaren reminisced. Carmine Martinez stepped forward to pay tribute to Valentino on behalf of the community of Hispanic actors. Then Rudy Vallee strode to the podium to offer his eulogy. In this, his third appearance, Vallee had quickly become a favorite with the crowd and was even asked to sing *The Sheik of Araby*, which Vallee politely declined to perform.

Throughout the remainder of the 1980's Bud Testa continued to draw upon the same people time and again. They were almost always welcomed by those attending the Valentino Memorial Service, even if their stories had long since been memorized by the audience, who listened politely year after year. These days, the only wild card was Estrellita. While she was never an invited speaker, her antics and unpredictable behavior at the crypt and during the service itself almost always stole the show.

In his opening prayer for the 1983 service, Reverend Pilson Potter offered God thanks for "Keeping the glitter of bright lights, like Rudy's, perpetually, Amen." Mary MacLaren again spoke of her times, and Rudy Vallee was again the featured speaker to offer the eulogy. This time, Vallee brought along his own amplification system, to the delight of those in the back rows. Vallee recalled seeing Valentino tango while on his Mineralava tour. "I've known myself some admiration from the fair sex, but I don't think any man has ever won the hearts of so many American women." Later Vallee was quoted in the press saying he thought Valentino's standing, albeit sadly, had faded with time, claiming "I don't think you'd find two out of five who would know who he was."

Estrellita felt that the timing was right to expand on her original story. For the sake of the press, she conveniently recalled that Valentino "Was crazy with love for my mother, and wanted to marry her." Claiming that her mother was only 15 at the time, she said that the family rejected the idea of an actor joining the family ranks, and undaunted, Rudy refused to take no for an answer, and had vowed to her mother 'I can wait.' Estrellita said death had robbed her mother of her true love. "She couldn't marry the man she loved. My mother loved Valentino in silence for what happened." Her mother had died ten years before, from complications stemming from a fall from a bus. Estrellita claimed that until that accident, her mother visited the Valentino crypt on a regular basis. Now, she claimed she was fulfilling a "Holy pledge" made to her mother, to come each week with white daisies to be placed on her mother's behalf, at Rudolph Valentino's grave.

Del Regil also expressed to reporters her anguish, as well as displeasure about where her mother was buried. "My sister made a mistake and put her up there" in Forest Lawn Cemetery. "I want to move her here, I'm going crazy thinking of my mother up there, not here." This was a commitment that Estrellita made to herself, and kept. She had her mother disinterred from Forest Lawn and relocated to Hollywood Memorial Park. Although all the facts line up to indicate that Estrellita's story of her mother's being the original Lady In Black is blatant fabrication, she holds the unique distinction of being the only alleged Lady In Black to be buried at the same cemetery as Valentino.

By August 1984 the Valentino Memorial was on automatic pilot. Bud Testa, himself aging, made very little effort to expand the services to bring in new blood. Again, the opening and closing prayer was led by Reverend Pilson Potter. One new face did turn up this year. African-American actor Lorenzo Tucker appeared this year, and recalled the early days in film and vaudeville. Tucker had never actually met Valentino, and his sole connection was in his being known as the Black Valentino.

Mary MacLaren, charming and beloved by everyone, was on hand, as usual, to offer her personal remembrances. Once again Norvell spoke and choose to repeat his previous years presentation on the reincarnation of Valentino. Vivian Duncan returned for a second time to provide the musical element. Rudy Vallee once more delivered the eulogy. The service was very brief and it's highly likely that most of the players had memorized their 'script' by this point. Ditra was correct when she warned Bud Testa that "It's time to change the script."

Now in a wheelchair, Mary MacLaren made her last appearance at the Valentino Memorial Services in 1984. Estrellita, holding a photo of her mother, stands behind Mary.

Crooner Rudy Vallee, left, greets Mary MacLaren, center, and Mike McKelvy, far right

157

February 23, 1984 marked a quiet end to Ditra Flame's long rein as the Lady In Black. She passed away quietly at her home on 613 Vesta Street in Ontario, California surrounded by Valentino memorabilia as well as a lifetime of memories. Now perhaps Ditra's soul could find peace, and possibly she was reunited with that dashing, handsome 24-year-old Italian immigrant she had befriended so very long ago, back in 1919. One thing was for certain. Outside of Valentino himself, Ditra Flame would prove to be the single most important participant in the history of the Valentino Memorial Services. Upon her 'retirement' in 1954, the services had never regained the zest or zeal she brought with her. After feeling a touch of nostalgia herself, she returned, in ordinary clothing, to be present at the 1965 and 1966 memorial services. Appropriately, her final appearance in 1977 was once again in full Lady In Black regalia. She had kept the faith, to the very end, to uphold his legacy, and try, in her own way, to perpetuate the name of Rudolph Valentino for generations to come. There is much room to criticize Ditra Flame, but at the same time she should be recognized as the most important person in the history of the Valentino Memorial Services. And now, that person was gone. Without fanfare, Ditra was laid to rest in her black dress, at the San Jacinto Valley Cemetery, and her gravestone, in addition to her name and dates, reads Lady In Black.

The 59th anniversary service on August 23, 1985 saw an influx in attendance. About 500 fans flocked to the 59th annual Valentino Memorial Service, and proclaiming it as one of "The largest crowds for the event in recent years," Bud Testa said "Each year the crowd seems to get a little bigger." Testa was truthful when he noted that "There's just no one like him. He had such a great charisma. He was such a magic person."

The lineup of speakers was predictable. The opening prayer was the familiar Troupers Chaplain, Pilson Potter. Next, a message from beloved Mary MacLaren was read. Those in attendance, who had grown not only fond of, but also accustomed to the annual appearance of Mary at the Valentino Memorial, were deeply concerned to learn of her recent hospitalization. All expressed their prayers for her, and wished her well. Thinking of the Valentino Memorial Service, Mary had sent ahead a note to be read to the audience, on her behalf. Then, once again, Norvell, acclaimed twentieth century philosopher, spoke yet again about the reincarnation of Valentino. Concluding the ceremony was the ever-popular Rudy Vallee.

The 60th Anniversary of the Valentino Memorial Services was marked by the loss of two veteran participants. On November 9, 1985, silent star Mary MacLaren succumbed at the age of 89. Another direct link to Valentino had been severed by death. And, just six weeks before the 6oth anniversary, Rudy Vallee passed away, at the age of 85, quietly at his home on July 3, 1986. And so, on August 23, 1986 those in attendance would see on their program Mike McKelvy, speaking for his first time, in a tribute to both Mary MacLaren and Rudy Vallee. McKelvy reminded the audience that Mary would "Delight you with her stories of being smothered with hugs and kisses when she had her dressing room next to him at Universal Studios."

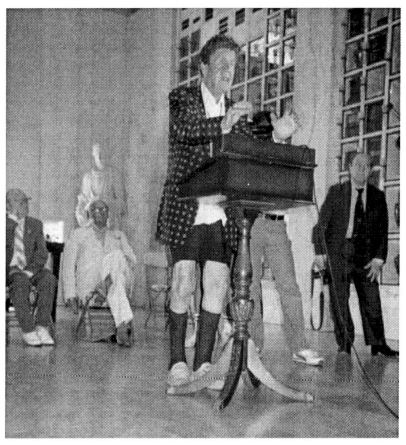

Rudy Vallee, sans his pants, gives the eulogy for the 1985 Valentino Memorial Service. This would be his final appearance as he died a month before the 1986 memorial service

The next speaker at the service would be Gaylord Carter, who recalled playing the organ for several of Valentino's silent films. Veteran MGM musical star, actress Virginia O'Brien concluded the services with her eulogy to Valentino's importance in film history. Rightfully labeling it "The biggest mistake they ever made," O'Brien alluded to Metro Studios letting Valentino slip through their grasp, over the issue of a small pay raise he had requested.

Estrellita, frustrated to find that she was but one of three Ladies In Black who showed up in 1986, was "doing some wailing of her own in a scenario every bit as melodramatic as anything Valentino ever performed. She tearfully and vehemently surveyed the other two Ladies In Black, one of whom was wearing a black pillbox hat, carrying a fake red rose, and wearing a blue "Welcome to Hollywood" button, the other (actually a man in drag) wearing a black fox fur hat with a veil as dense as a damask tablecloth. She called them sacrilegious, 'monkeys' and 'phonies'

160

who were 'offending the memory of my mother. I am furious, I am in a rage,' she verbally stormed as someone put a restraining arm around her. 'You come here to love and respect. They're coming for publicity.' Her black mantilla swirling about her, she angrily tore from the two vases on Valentino's tomb, all the red roses and carnations others had left there, everything except the white daisies, symbolizing the bunch that appeared on the table at the New York restaurant where she said Valentino and her mother, Marquesa Di Lara, had dined sixty years ago."

While never on the program, and for just cause, Estrellita never the less could always manage to divert all attention to her direction. This year she was in full force by decorating the marble corridor leading to Valentino's crypt with large black stars made of paper, and on each Rudolph Valentino's name was spelled out in gold glitter. A single red rose was laid across each star. Anyone taking the path to visit Rudy's resting-place would find a whole layout of blankets, knick-knacks and photos that she had displayed in the alcove adjacent to Rudy's crypt.

Services for the 61st anniversary were held in accordance with the tradition of having the memorial the following day if the 23rd fell on a Sunday. The lineup included the opening prayer offered once again by Pilson Potter, and Eleanor Vallee spoke at the services this year on behalf of her late husband, Rudy Vallee. She spoke of his relationship with, and fondness for participating in the Valentino Memorial Services. Mike McKelvy chose to speak about Pola Negri and told of her final days in the hospital and how she had filled out her admittance form listing herself as a retired actress. Towards the end, with her doctor assisting her, she raised up from her bed and cried out "I was the greatest film actress in the world." It would prove to be Pola's final performance, as she passed away on August 1, 1987. Bob Mitchell who was the founder of the famous Bob Mitchell's Boys Choir, spoke for the first time, on how he played for silent films including those of Valentino. Lenore Miller who served as president of the Troupers Club spoke of Valentino as a neighbor. Suzanne Valentino who claimed to be a first cousin twice removed sang a song in tribute. Actor Dean Dittman offered brief remarks on legends that live on.

Halloween? No, it's the 1986 Valentino Memorial Service. An unidentified man dressed as the Lady In Black, left, and a man in Indian attire, joined the sincere for the 60th anniversary of the Valentino Memorial Service

Estrellita placed black stars with Valentino's name in glitter, with a red rose all the way down the corridor leading to the Valentino crypt. Circa August 23,1986

View of the audience at the 1986 Valentino Memorial Service

Estrellita taped roses to the Valentino crypt as well as surrounding crypts with black electrical tape
Circa 1986

Estrellita visits the Valentino grave after the 1986 memorial service

165

Actress Virginia O'Brien is interviewed on the mausoleum steps as Bud Testa, center, with hands on hips talks to a Valentino admirer. Circa 1986

Campy sheik costumes plagued the 1986 Valentino Memorial

Veteran MGM musical performer Virginia O'Brien gave the keynote address for the 1986
Valentino Memorial Service

Estrellita set up a shrine to not only Valentino, but her mother as well. Here she displays her mother's items on the window sill next to Valentino's grave. Circa 1988

The services begin to have an uneven, haphazard quality, and unfortunately would continue in this format until the late 1990's. For the 1988 Valentino Memorial Services, John Kelley was the new Trouper's Chaplain and gave the opening prayer. Bob Mitchell again gave his remembrances, and Joe Wagstaff gave a eulogy for Valentino on behalf of the Film Welfare League. Dean Dittman, perhaps thinking nobody would notice, repeated his spiel about how Valentino ties in with legends that live on.

The real treat was the first and only time appearance of silent film star Mary Philbin (*Phantom of the Opera* with Lon Chaney). A soft-spoken 86-year-old lady, her remarks were very brief, as she recalled Rudy as "a fine actor and a true gentleman." Due to the inept microphone system, a majority of the audience couldn't hear her. Impolitely, they began to yell, "we can't hear you" while she was still speaking, thus overriding her voice even for those seated closest to the podium. Mary Philbin appeared startled, yet trudged forward and concluded remarks by saying "Thank you for inviting me to this event, and God Bless you." She was gracious to remain afterwards to sign autographs for any who requested. In addition to personally knowing Rudolph, Mary Philbin had attended the Valentino funeral in New York and Los Angeles in 1926.

The final memorial service for the decade saw a similar lineup to previous years. Mike McKelvy articulated a salute to Valentino's leading lady in his last two films, Vilma Banky, who was still alive, at the age of 86. The only new speakers for the 1989 memorial were actress Mady Maguire who was invited to speak of an unnamed Valentino film project but ended up with a long dissertation on her own career. The other new face was the talented opera singer, Ken Remo. He sang two songs *The Sheik of Araby*, which was ironic since Rudolph Valentino had despised any association with that particular song. His second selection was one closer to Rudy's liking, considering that Valentino himself had recorded it, called *The Kashmiri Love Song*. Remo had a distinguished career which included guest appearances on classic television shows such as *The Tennessee Ernie Ford Show* and *The Loretta Young S*how. He also was an MGM recording artist his *Mexico* appeared on the Cash Box list of hits. Remo and his tenor voice were always a welcome addition to the Valentino Memorial.

Silent film star Mary Philbin shown here circa 1924

Legendary *Phantom of the Opera* star Mary Philbin briefly addresses the 1988
Valentino Memorial Service

Beloved silent star Mary Philbin makes a rare public appearance on behalf of the
Valentino Memorial Service, August 23, 1988

Universal Pictures silent star Mary Philbin fields a question as she is interviewed at the
conclusion of the 1988 Valentino Memorial Services

Mary Philbin, 86, graciously answers questions pertaining to her attending the Valentino funeral
in New York (1926), as well as discussing the upcoming Andrew Lloyd Webber stage musical
based on the *Phantom of the Opera*.

Estrellita decorated the Valentino crypt and alcove in what appeared to be New Years Eve style, with confetti and party streamers for the 1989 Valentino Memorial Service.

Mike McKelvy speaks on Valentino's leading lady Vilma Banky at the 1989
Valentino Memorial Service

Ken Remo sings *The Sheik of Araby* at the 1989 Valentino Memorial Service

1990 – 1999

The dullness that plagued the Valentino Memorial Services throughout the previous decade would unfortunately continue a while longer. Those in charge, namely Bud Testa, seemed bored and lacked any imagination or fresh ideas to bring to the services. Hollywood Memorial Park Cemetery in the past had underwritten the minimal cost of hosting each years services began to experience financial difficulties. Jack Roth, the owner whom Ditra Flame had found to be such a "gruff individual" was now in his 90's and it was later discovered that he had allegedly embezzled the endowment care funds that had been set aside for the perpetual upkeep of the cemetery grounds and buildings. Each year the cemetery shockingly fell into a deeper state of disrepair. In the Cathedral Mausoleum several of the skylights had cracked and broken away, letting rain stream in. Even the stained glass windows were broken in several places, including the one in the Valentino alcove. Cobwebs and dirt became commonplace in the corridors and it was obvious that no upkeep of any sort was being maintained within the mausoleum.

Valentino Memorial Service audience August 23, 1990

Estrellita poses once again with a large floral tribute to Rudolph Valentino at the 1990
Valentino Memorial Service

176

Through all this adversity, the Valentino Memorial, although not flourishing, would continue to limp along. Most everyone who knew Valentino personally had long vanished from the scene. Testa now had to rely on people who had written books, or claimed a connection to the Valentino lineage, whether it be real or imagined. By now, the only thing that brought excitement to the services was the ever-unpredictable Estrellita Del Regil. She continued to pace the corridors each year, sometimes suddenly demanding for no apparent reason, that various people be thrown out, but of course her demands were ignored. In fact, her rash, erratic behavior had many people wanting *her* expelled from future services. She continued with her theme decorating each year. For August 23, 1990 she had cut white paper into the shape of a heart, and using red glitter she inscribed on each one, the phrase "My Heart Belongs to Daddy" and then taped a piece of wrapped butterscotch candy on top of each heart.

The service itself, with an estimated 200 people in attendance witnessed the kick off of the final decade of the century. As standard custom, John Kelley opened in an appropriate prayer. Next, a moment in silence was set aside to commemorate the memory of past long-time revered participants Mary MacLaren and Rudy Vallee. Again, Bob Mitchell recalled his playing for Valentino's films, and how as young adults they would emulate Valentino's hairstyle to the dismay of their mothers who attempted in vain to wash the Vaseline from their pillowcases. Mike McKelvy spoke on another of Valentino's leading ladies. This year he selected Gloria Swanson, who had starred in *Beyond the Rocks* with Valentino in 1922. Also included in the lineup was an Argentine actress named Argentina Brunetti, who discussed her film work as well as her claim to a close friendship with the Valentino family. A simple prayer by Troupers' Chaplain John Kelley concluded the 1990 services on a proper note.

For the memorial service of 1991 the lineup included Jack Scagnetti, who was author of *The Intimate Life of Rudolph Valentino*. Scagnetti spoke of the in-depth research for his book and his access to Luther Mahoney's first hand observations while working for Valentino at both of his residences, the Whitley Heights and

Falcon Lair estates. Mike McKelvy spoke once more, this time on Patsy Ruth Miller, who had a supporting role in the 1921 Valentino version of *Camille*. Also repeating his remembrances was Bob Mitchell. Paul Valentine was there to offer a reading that Bud Testa stated was "Appropriate for this memorial." However when Valentine took to the podium he was dressed in apparel that tried to imitate a sheik's garb it yet looked closer to pajama material. Once again the Valentino Memorial Services fell victim to self-serving buffoonery.

Rounding out the service, Bob Mitchell presented his Boy's Choir to sing two songs, one associated with the Valentino film *Blood and Sand* called *The Toreador Song*. Once again Estrellita Del Regil stole the show by concocting a big drama at the Valentino crypt. With great flair she removed the floral arrangements placed earlier in both urns that flank his grave and swiftly threw them to the floor, and stomped on them. Then, she triumphantly placed her own flowers in the dual urns. As the years rolled on, the story of her mother being the original Lady In Black seemed to recede more and more into the background, as Estrellita's role grew more prominent. Many in the press simply identified her as being the original Lady In Black, and she got so caught up in her role that she neglected to correct their omission of her mother.

Estrellita wasn't the only one stomping at Valentino's grave. It was reported earlier in the year that King of Pop Michael Jackson made frequent secret night time visits and practiced many of his famous dance steps right there in front of the Valentino crypt. It's quite possible that he felt Valentino's spirit would reach out to inspire him, or maybe teach him the tango. Talk about a "Thriller."

The next several years were lean ones indeed for the memorial service. Bud Testa invited the same fatigued speakers year after year. Due to this, attendance started to dramatically wane. Those who had been attending the services for a number of years had gotten to hear, and meet people who actually knew Rudolph Valentino.

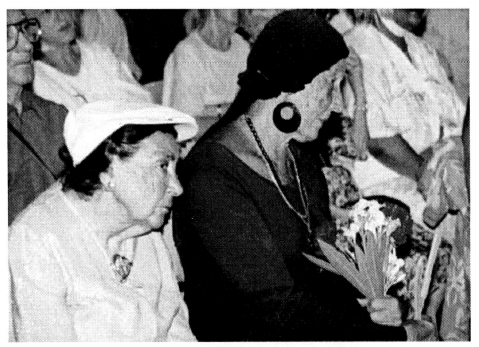

Estrellita, dressed in black at the 1991 Valentino Memorial Service. Her sister sits to her left

A bowl of white daisies that Estrellita said represented the flowers on the table of the dinner her mother had with
Valentino (which was fabrication)

Bob Mitchell speaks at the 1990 Valentino Memorial Service

180

Now they were all gone, and the people who were invited to speak were telling the same stories over and over. Some felt that if they missed any particular given year they could come back the next and hear the same presentation.

One notable difference occurred in 1994 when Estrellita Del Regil failed to appear. Age had caught up with her, and at 89 years of age, due to health problems, she was kept from continuing her annual excursion to the Valentino Memorial Service.

In 1995 yet another Lady In Black materialized upon the scene. Vicki Callahan attempted to pick up the torch that Estrellita had enjoyed for so long. Callahan actually had a type of Valentino connection of her own. Attending school at Eagle Rock Junior High, she enrolled in a drama class that was taught by Walter Craig. Craig, who in movies was billed as Anthony Dexter, was most famous for his portrayal of Valentino in the 1951 movie. She maintained a lifetime friendship with the former actor, and that association caused her to seek out more about the real Valentino. Self billed as the "3rd generation Lady In Black," she would help continue to perpetuate the tradition of having a Lady In Black in attendance by appearing in her black dress and with her black handbag, the name 'Rudolph Valentino' spelled out in silver glitter or rhinestones. Although she never wore any veil as had previous Ladies In Black, she did sport a black wig on some of her appearances.

The year 1995 marked the centennial of the birth of Rudolph Valentino. Salutes around the world were held, including his hometown of Castellaneta. A film festival took place in conjunction with the occasion, and a small museum had been dedicated. Renowned silent film historian Kevin Brownlow and David Gill jointly oversaw the restoration of *The Four Horseman of the Apocalypse* complete with a rousing Carl Davis score, which was released just in time for the centennial celebration.

Unfortunately, however, things were going from bad to worse on the Valentino Memorial home front. For the first time in their history, the 1996 services were removed from Hollywood Memorial Park Cemetery to the Silent Movie Theater at 611 Fairfax Avenue. The mausoleum remained open and a small handful of devoted fans gathered to hold an impromptu prayer at Rudy's crypt before joining the official services at the Silent Movie Theater. Once there, the audience was seated in an air-conditioned building, offering a nice perk that the Cathedral Mausoleum never had the luxury of, on all those sweltering hot August memorials. Bud Testa announced that the service was held there through the courtesy of proprietor Larry Austin. The lineup for the 70th anniversary included Mike McKelvy who continued his tradition of speaking on Valentino's leading ladies, choosing Katherine MacDonald who had played opposite him in a pre-star film entitled *Passions Playground* in 1920. McKelvy noted that MacDonald was "The sister of our late beloved friend, Mary MacLaren."

Diane Whitmore, left, joins Vicki Callahan in front of the grave of Rudolph Valentino on August 23, 1996

Another interesting speaker was Bob Williams, whose father operated a shop directly across the street from Campbell's Funeral Church. He vividly recalled his impressions as a young boy back in August 1926, of the pandemonium he witnessed while gazing out of the window, watching the continuous crush of crowds attempting to view the Valentino bier.

Larry Austin also spoke about his mother being a seamstress for the Valentino film *The Eagle* and hinted that perhaps she knew some secrets that she had taken to her grave, as he told the audience that in those days you didn't tell what you knew, if you wanted to keep your job. Ken Remo once again was a crowd pleaser in his two traditional numbers. With improved acoustics, rather than the echoing marble halls of the mausoleum, Remo was able to shine this year more than ever. Patricia Lampinen who was the editor of the Valentino Newsletter read a couple of selections of poems from Valentino's book *Day Dreams*. Marc Wanamaker also spoke of the Valentino era. Again, Bob Mitchell spoke and presented his Boy's Choir. The 70th memorial was closed with a prayer.

Just a couple weeks later, on September 22, 1996, Jean G. Valentino, the last living direct family link to Valentino passed away at the age of 82. Doted on by Rudy as a youth, he carved out a career of his own by becoming an Emmy Award-winning sound engineer, working on various television classics such as Bewitched, Rawhide, Petticoat Junction and Father Knows Best. His connection to the Valentino Memorial Service went back to almost the very beginning. His first attendance was with his father, in 1928 at the age of 14. Although he later joined forces with his father, Alberto to decry the "carnivals and slapstick" events held each anniversary at the crypt, he would continue to show up now and again at some of the services throughout the years. The loss of the last remaining family member who heard the sound of Rudolph Valentino's voice, and knew him so well, indeed marked the end of an era.

With the cemetery in such a precarious financial state, Valentino fans didn't know what to expect for the 1997 memorial. It was now standard for the cemetery to keep the mausoleum totally locked on Saturdays. The fact that the Valentino Memorial fell on a Saturday this year had no impact on the front office. Bud Testa made the abrupt decision to hold the memorial on Friday, August 22, 1997. With only word of mouth and scant (if any) publicity, the 71st Valentino Memorial Services returned to their origin. Bud Testa opened the services and mentioned the shortage of funds and beseeched the crowd to contribute $5.00 each, so they could rent chairs for next year's service. There were about seven chairs there, which were for the use of the guest speakers. All others had to stand as the service unfolded. Most in attendance on that day figured they were witnessing the final hurrah in the long history of the Valentino Memorial. Any mourners who arrived the next day, assuming that the services were always held on the actual day, August 23rd, would be startled to find the mausoleum doors padlocked, with various floral offerings piled at the foot of the secured doors.

The year 1998 would be a pivotal one to the annual Valentino Memorial. In the early part of the year the cemetery, sinking deeper into disrepair, caused most to wonder how long the downward spiral could continue. It was later revealed that Hollywood Memorial Park Cemetery, under the ownership of Jack Roth, in the previous two years had made more money from families disinterring their deceased loved ones, than they made for actual funerals held there. Now with the state of California involved, the cemetery was deemed financially insolvent, and found itself on the auction block. Tyler Cassity remembered hearing of the availability of this legendary cemetery in early 1998 while in the Los Angeles area for a presentation of his "Forever" biography concept at a gathering at Rose Hills cemetery. Before long, with a sealed bid of only $375,000.00 Tyler Cassity along with his partner and brother, Brent found their bid accepted and themselves at the helm of the 'Cemetery of the Immortals.' Tyler Cassity foresaw typical funerals being turned into enduring legacies. He stated he wanted to fill in the dash between the dates of birth and death. Through audio-video technology he planned to bring the near one hundred-year-old cemetery into the digital age. A place where not only the famous, but the everyday beloved grandmothers and grandfathers could, in effect, speak out, in their own words for generations to come, where their great grandchildren could activate a few buttons at the kiosk and hear their long departed relatives reach out and tell of their experiences, and share with generations of family yet born, the joys, sorrows and heartbreaks that they had endured. Such a concept was truly revolutionary for the funeral industry.

The 1998 services themselves were again mundane and repetitive; the lineup included Bob Mitchell who introduced Patrick Valentino who played a piece at the piano. Mike McKelvy spoke of Nita Naldi, Valentino's notorious co-star in both *Blood and Sand* as well as *Cobra* and *A Sainted Devil.* Author of *The Intimate Life of Rudolph Valentino*, Jack Scagnetti was once again on hand to give an overview of Valentino's career. Again, Patricia Lampinen, who had founded the *Rudolph Valentino Newsletter*, read a selection of poems from Valentino's book *Day Dreams.*

The surprise element of 1998 was the appearance of Estrellita Del Regil, ushered in by Mike McKelvy. Old timers, who remembered her glory days at the Valentino Memorial Services, welcomed her once more, although this time, she was wheelchair bound. At the age of 93, delighted to be there, she clapped her hands as she was wheeled down the isle, saying "Long time no see. Long time no see." So-called third generation Lady In Black Vicki Callahan rose from her seat to warmly greet her predecessor. Ladies In Black from past and present had come together.

Those who wandered about prior to the service would notice a stark change in the appearance of the mausoleum. The entire marble flooring had been noticeably polished and all the cobwebs dust and dirt had vanished.

Clear evidence of a change of regime – polished marble floors and rented folding chairs for guests at the 1998 Valentino Memorial Service

It was as if the place had taken on a new life. While it would remain a while before the skylights and stained glass windows would see repair, the wheels of change were clearly evident. Everyone who embraced and cherished the Valentino Memorial Service as one of the last vestiges of grand Hollywood traditions, breathed a huge sigh of relief knowing that under the respectful direction of Tyler Cassity it would, indeed persevere.

But on August 23, 1998 very few knew who Tyler was. He chose to remain in the background, and unannounced. Content to observe, and take in just what the Valentino Memorial Service was about. Perhaps he was attempting to find what was behind this most unique event, that extended far longer than the life span of those who actually know Rudolph Valentino. Although Cassity wasn't well known to the attendees just yet, within a short time it would become probable that by his purchase of the cemetery, he helped revitalize the Valentino Memorial Service.

Just two years earlier, less than twenty people had shown up for the Valentino Memorial Service. And those twenty that were there saw the cemetery grounds as well as the Cathedral Mausoleum in a horrible, shocking state of neglect. For the service there had been no seats for the guests, and Bud Testa had to actually beseech the crowd for donations of any size, in order to keep the flame of the memorial burning. Now, on August 23, 1999, for the final memorial service of the twentieth century, the guests arrived, finding a host of cemetery staff buzzing about, fixing the final details of the service. Curtains had been hung over the unused door that was directly opposite the main entrance. Over the curtain hung an impressive oversize charcoal drawing bust of Rudolph Valentino in his *Son of the Sheik* pose. It was drawn specifically for the Valentino Memorial by artist Jonathan Morell. Everywhere there were sound engineers, cameramen and their assistants. Portions of the service were to be recorded for an HBO documentary *The Young and the Dead.*

Tyler Cassity poses on the front steps of the Cathedral Mausoleum after the 1998 Valentino Memorial Service

New signage for the renamed cemetery. Formerly called Hollywood Memorial Park Cemetery, in 1998 it was renamed Hollywood Forever Cemetery

Estrellita was once again wheeled in for the Valentino Memorial Service, from her rest home in La Mirada. Holding a single red rose, and dressed in black, she remained silent as she watched the furor of activity unfurl around her. Tyler Cassity stepped out from the sidelines and took to the podium to officially open the service. Blessed with striking good looks and a voice to match, Cassity projected a warmth and easy demeanor as he spoke, putting everyone instantly at ease. In welcoming the huge crowd for his very first time, he expressed his desire that "We have done you proud this year." This brought forth a spontaneous burst of applause from the crowd. With this instant seal of approval now secure, Tyler introduced something new to the Valentino Memorials. A huge projection screen was set up and a "Forever Tribute" was shown. This consisted of a montage of photos and film clips set to an instrumental version of the title song of the 1951 *Valentino* film. This new addition was quite entertaining and found acceptance with the crowd. As the film ended it showed his dates of birth and death. Surprisingly, the cemetery where Valentino rested had somehow gotten his year of death wrong, listing it as 1923 instead of the proper date of 1926.

Bud Testa who was unable to be present at the opening of the service had pre-recorded an introduction to what would be on the program. Mark Wanamaker spoke at length of Valentino's time in Hollywood, also mentioning the new management's efforts to restore the former glory to the cemetery. He then informed the crowd that Valentino's home, Falcon Lair had just been sold, and the new owner, Thomas Blount, respected the history of the legendary estate, and intended to fully restore it. Wanamaker suggested that the crowd should give a round of applause to him for having the keen foresight to save Falcon Lair from the wrecking ball. Applause was swift, even without Thomas Blount being there to accept the affirmation of the crowd.

Actor Michael Goodwin then spoke, reading a passage from the book *My Private Diary*. Next up was famous psychic to the stars Kenny Kingston who charmed the crowd by having everyone in the mausoleum turn around and greet the person behind them and say something nice. He told of a night at the theater in Italy during the mid 1940's as the guest of Doris Duke who confessed to him in a private moment that although she was listed as the richest woman in the world, the only man she wanted a romantic involvement with was Rudolph Valentino, and he was dead. Kingston pointed out how ironic it was that Duke, a few years after this admission, had purchased the Valentino Falcon Lair estate and that she had even passed away there. He then closed his elegant remarks by speaking a phrase in Italian, when translated was something he said we all would say to Valentino on this occasion of his memorial – "I shall love you for all my life, and please have sweet dreams." And he insisted that Rudy, were he able to answer, would say in return, "Thank you for coming."

Silent film fan Mike McKelvy announced that this was his twentieth year of attending the memorial and that he had first come with beloved Mary MacLaren. This year he spoke of Doris Kenyon who had costarred with Valentino in the 1924 motion picture *Monsieur Beaucaire*. As McKelvy was finishing his remarks, Bud Testa was ushered in to a place of honor behind the podium. McKelvy was to introduce the next speaker who was Vicki Callahan the "3rd Generation Lady In Black." Before she stepped forward, McKelvy gave Estrellita a brief moment of recognition, calling her "The old Lady In Black." Callahan read a note on behalf of the producers of *Valentino – The Musical* and played a selection from their production. Next Ken Remo sang his traditional two songs, to the delight of the audience. Remo could always be counted on to bring the house down with his powerful voice.

Psychic to the stars, Kenny Kingston speaks fondly of Doris Duke at the 1999 Valentino Memorial Service

Estrellita Del Regil poses with Vicki Callahan at the 1999 Valentino Memorial Service

Michael Goodwin co-star in television's *Eight Is Enough* series, stepped forward again and read three selections of poetry from Valentino's book of poems called *Daydreams*. The selections he read were *Sympathy, Co-operation* and *Remembrance*. Then to close the occasion Tyler Cassity acknowledged the "Life force behind this service," Bud Testa, and suggested the guests should give him an standing ovation. Testa slowly waved back to the crowd as the applause filled the corridors. Then without the usual benefit of a closing prayer, the services abruptly concluded.

Tyler Cassity initiated two other unique projects. Beginning this year, Hollywood Forever Cemetery started an annual tradition of hosting an outdoor screening of a Valentino motion picture free of charge. This year *Son of the Sheik* was shown the night before the memorial service. Well attended, the screening allowed people to sit on the chairs provided or bring blankets and enjoy the presentation. The second project was more in line with the core business of the company, but with a Valentino twist to it. An entire wing of cremation niches was being offered for those who wished to be buried in close proximity to Rudolph Valentino. Called 'The Valentino Shrine' the cemetery prepared advance brochures showing what it would look like upon completion, and even offered pre-construction price discounts.

2000 - 2003

The first Valentino Memorial of the new century was packed with attendees who saw the beautiful red and white carnations on vivid display to the left of the podium. A full-length painting by Christopher Jones was done, in full color, of Valentino in the *Son of the Sheik* attire, and was propped up against the back curtains. The service was opened once again by Bud Testa, who, in failing health had made it to the service, and introduced Tyler Cassity who noted that as he looked out at the crowd, it was "Inspiring to see such a full house." With his unique flair he closed, saying a "Thank you for your dedication." Cassity also paid homage to Estrellita Del Regil, by saying "It wouldn't be quite the same event if we didn't have Estrellita here," and thanked her for coming. Sadly, this would prove to be her last appearance. This colorful Lady In Black would pass away a short five months later on January 28, 2001 at the age of 96. Again, it was the end of an era. By this time it didn't matter that Estrellita's claims weren't true. As a lively participant of the Valentino Memorial, her eccentric antics would be discussed long after she departed the scene.

Again, the cemetery showed the same "Forever Tribute" and as it unfolded those who had been there the year before wondered if they had at least corrected the error in the date of death. But at the conclusion, it showed the same date. It was a small price to pay, perhaps, for the improvements everyone was witnessing.

Bud Testa introduced Reverend Howe of Toluca Lake. In a welcomed return to tradition, once again a clergyman opened the service in prayer. Next came Mike McKelvy who spoke of Clara Kimball Young, whose 1919 motion picture *Eyes of Youth* had provided Valentino the major break in his career. Next, Valentino biographer Emily Leider took to the podium to speak on the importance of June Mathis. She touched on the fact that it was Mathis who first saw leading man quality in Valentino. And that it was she alone who had stepped forward and provided what was then deemed to be a temporary resting-place, that of course later turned permanent. Jimmy Bangley then arose to discuss the numerous colleagues and friends of Valentino's who were also buried at various places within the cemetery grounds. Bangley also added his praise regarding the turnaround of the appearance of the cemetery, and injected that he felt that "Rudy is happy too."

Valentino archivist Jim Craig then recited three selections of poems from *Day Dreams*. He read *Heart Flower*, *Mirage*, and *At Sunrise To-morrow*. Writer Lisa Mitchell then arose to read an article she wrote in 1976 for the *Los Angeles Times*. Randall Herold then provided the musical element, by singing a cappella *The Desert Song*. His voice was quite impressive, and the a cappella angle, made it unique. Reverend Howe then came forward to conclude the service with a prayer and said that "In affirming Valentino, we also validate our own gifts."

At the conclusion of the service the cemetery offered complimentary souvenir digital photos to be posed in front of the Valentino crypt. What appeared as a generous gesture turned into a unique marketing ploy. When they were later called to pick up their digital photo, they would be given a soft sales pitch suggesting purchasing pre-need arrangements.

The 75th anniversary of the Valentino Memorial Service would see a major revitalization from the Testa years. With ill health preventing Bud Testa from taking part, new cemetery owner Tyler Cassity took a firm grasp in charting the Valentino Memorial's direction. Guests arriving were presented a single red rose to place in memory of Rudolph, at his crypt, where large clear glass containers were stationed. Unfortunately no one told the attendees of the plan, and it was found at the conclusion of the service that no more than seven roses had been deposited in the designated vases.

When arrivals entered the main corridor of the Cathedral Mausoleum they found decorative greenery surrounding the doorway with a '7' and '5' flanking each side of the entry doors respectively. One would have to have gone back as far as the 1920's to witness such lavish floral demonstrations.

Tyler Cassity, appeared visibly astonished at the sheer size of the anniversary crowds and opened with "Wow... look at this room...incredible 75 years later!" It instantly set the tone. Without further ado Tyler introduced both Charles Mandracchia, and Diane Salfalzone, who sang a song from the upcoming Broadway production of *Valentino – The Musical.* The song was called *Romance Will Stand the Test of Time.* With years of amateur talent forced upon them at previous Valentino Memorials, the crowd went wild with appreciation for a Valentino number presented with Broadway quality. Next on the program would be a new video presentation called 'A Tribute to Valentino.'

Tyler Cassity welcomes guests at the 75th anniversary Valentino
Memorial Services, August 23, 2001

Jeanie Villalobos, great niece of Rudolph Valentino poses with Melodie Shorey
at the 75th anniversary of the Valentino Memorial Service

195

Diane Salfalzone and Charles Mandracchia open the 75th anniversary Valentino
Memorial Services with a musical number from their Broadway show

It was a montage of Valentino photos, narrated by Hollywood Forever historian Annette Lloyd. If anyone had checked the program, they would have noticed that Bud Testa was listed as the next speaker, to discuss the highlights of past memorial services. Sadly, due to declining health, this year would mark the first year that Testa was unable to attend since he had started almost a half century ago. Stepping in at the last minute were Anton Gazenbeek and Yoko Nakijana. As a team they performed a unique and entertaining demonstration of the tango dance, so vividly connected to the legend of Rudolph Valentino.

Hollywood historian Marc Wanamaker then took to the podium to address how Valentino fit in as a cultural icon of 1920's America. Rick Larson, backed on the organ by Bob Mitchell, sang the two traditional numbers, *The Sheik of Araby* and *The Kashmiri Song*. Then, making his second consecutive appearance, Jimmy Bangley told the audience that he was "Thrilled, pleased and proud to be here." Giving a unique perspective on the Valentino method of acting, Bangley drew upon his former neighbor, film legend Bette Davis who told him she "Got his message loud and clear." He mentioned how Davis had confided in him that she sat through *The Four Horseman of the Apocalypse* five times, transfixed by Valentino's acting. "He was a great actor" Bette Davis recalled. No one in the audience on this day would dispute her findings.

Tyler Cassity reclaimed the podium to acknowledge a couple of people from the audience, including Famous Players Lasky (Paramount) founder's daughter, Betty Lasky. Saying it "Looks like we have a Lady In White" Tyler made mention of the attire of Diane Whitmore, indicating, although wrongly, she was upholding a tradition of Ditra Flame. Jim Craig was next up, and again read two short poems from the book of poetry Valentino had published in 1923. *Faithfulness* and *Dust to Dust* were his chosen selections. Next, Craig introduced to those attending, the niece of June Mathis, Diane Madsen, and then the great grand niece of Rudolph Valentino, Jeanine Villalobos. The knowledge that June Mathis and Rudolph Valentino lay in permanent rest next to each other, and that their respective nieces' had simultaneously attended this anniversary, added a historic touch to

197

the 75th Valentino Memorial Service. There is no evidence that any Mathis relatives had ever previously attended any of the Valentino Memorial Services.

To conclude the ceremony Tyler Cassity spoke tongue in cheek, saying that "I hope to see you all at the 100th anniversary which I am sure we will be having... and the way you can guarantee that, is to purchase your own cremation niche..." The crowd roared and then to cap off the end of the service, the *Valentino – The Musical* stars once again were ushered in to perform their final song *Only Your Love*. When the number was over the sound of applause and cheers was unequaled. Co-creator Francesca Digiosa came forward from behind the screen where she had been overseeing the music background, and joined hands with Charles and Diana and locked hand in hand, all three took a well-deserved bow. And so, after 75 years, the Valentino Memorial had achieved a dramatic turnaround. Just a couple of years earlier the fate of the service had been in jeopardy. Now, not only was it ready to continue but the numbers attending were escalating.

Perhaps due to all the excitement of the 75th memorial, the greatest oversight was the failure to announce that Estrellita had passed away at the age of 96 on January 28th of that year. At her final appearance the previous year, Tyler himself had acknowledged, "It wouldn't be the same without Estrellita." Now, she was gone, and no mention was made.

The volume of people attending the August 23, 2002, Valentino Memorial Service seemed to again astound Hollywood Forever owner Tyler Cassity. He introduced himself in his welcoming remarks, which started at the traditional time of exactly at 12:10 p.m. "Thank you all for coming, this is amazing... look at this crowd – 76 years after Valentino died!" Tyler went on to express his appreciation by saying "Thank you for keeping the faith and keeping this going. Each year I think will this be the year no one comes... and each year there is more of you!" Cassity summed it up as a "Fantastic tribute to Valentino" and the 76th Valentino Memorial was under way.

Lady In White, Diane Whitmore searches for a seat at the 75th anniversary Valentino Memorial Service

Tammie Kadin views the special 75th Valentino Memorial decorations that adorn the front doors of the Cathedral Mausoleum

Great niece of June Mathis, Diane Madsen poses between her great Aunt's crypt, and that of
Rudolph Valentino at the 75th anniversary of the Valentino Memorial Service

Lobby cards on display at the Valentino Memorial Service 2002

Fans gather in front of the Valentino crypt on August 23, 2002

Cemetery employee and silent film devotee Annette Lloyd took to the podium and spoke of the "Endurance of the star power and appeal" of Valentino. She then introduced what was becoming standard fare under the Tyler rein, that being a new mini video on Valentino each year. This year's video segment touted the 'Romance of Valentino' and set to sweeping music various clips of romantic moments from a handful of his films. This year Tyler changed the format slightly from the previous year, and reinstated Bud Testa's tradition of individually introducing each speaker. Previously Tyler had spoken only at the opening and closing of the service.

Marc Wanamaker once again spoke of Valentino's place in Hollywood and recalled some of the details of the chaos of the New York funeral as well as the grieving across the nation. Although a few of his facts were wrong, Wanamaker expressed a deep love for the Valentino era in Hollywood, and this was not lost on the audience.

"With 76 years there is so much tradition and this event has evolved so much. This will be the first year since 1951 that Bud Testa will not be here." Having said that, Tyler asked the audience to make the service this year a tribute to Testa whom Cassity extolled as the "Man who made it happen for the last fifty years."

Tradition was resurrected when a purposely unidentified Lady In Black, arrived, and whom Tyler introduced as the next speaker. She briefly covered the saga surrounding the legend of all the Ladies In Black, and concluded her remarks by saluting her predecessors, saying "They gave their time, and their roses to Rudolph Valentino." Karie Bible was deemed a 'new' Lady In Black. She brought back the original tradition of keeping her veil on, thus returning the mystique to the legend of the Lady In Black. Providing his own special magic, Ken Remo once again returned to sing the double standards by now so closely associated not only with Valentino, but with the Valentino Memorial Service as well. He was accompanied by organist Bob Mitchell.

Los Angeles Times reporter Susan Compo then read an article that she had written about the Valentino Memorial in 1986. Then, ever entertaining Jimmy Bangley enlightened those attending the 76th memorial with his discussion of Valentino as a sex symbol. Preaching to the choir, Bangley broke no new ground by telling the audience that "He was not called the world's greatest lover for nothing. And no one ever surpassed him." While in the midst of his remarks, serious feedback from the microphone system filled the mausoleum corridor. Without missing a beat, Bangley looked upwards to the left and right and quickly suggested in jest that we were getting "Interference from Pola Negri!" His quick wit and ad libbing brought roars to the house and provided it with one of its funniest moments of the year.

Jimmy Bangley is interviewed by the press next to the Valentino Shrine on August 23, 2002

Tyler then introduced actor Michael Goodwin to read selected poetry from *Day Dreams*. However, for reasons unknown, Goodwin instead choose to read a long drawn out passage from *My Private Diary* which was a book put out after Valentino's death that drew from his European travels in 1923.

Valentino Forever author Tracy Terhune prepares to speak at the 76th anniversary Valentino Memorial Service

To conclude the services on a solemn note, Tracy Terhune was introduced and a vintage recording of *There's A New Star In Heaven Tonight* was played. The song was written just days after Valentino had died in 1926. It became an instant success with the public. It appeared on piano rolls, sheet music and several artists saw fit to record it on various phonograph record labels. Amazingly, this year would mark the first time it had ever been played at the Valentino Memorial Services. After the song I spoke briefly about the history of the Valentino Memorial Services stating we owed a great "Debt of gratitude" to those who had kept the service going the previous 76 years, for "Caring and carrying on." Then, with a reading of the actual prayer card that was distributed at the door of the Church of the Good Shepherd on the day of Valentino's funeral, September 7, 1926, the services concluded. It was a successful balance; a mix of readings, songs and prayerful reflection.

The skies above were bright and clear, and the palm trees that line the cemetery streets had a sight sway to them as they yielded to a gentle breeze blowing on the day of the 77th Anniversary. Noon-time temperatures inching up to the low 90's greeted attendees to the 2003 Valentino Memorial Services.

Author of *Dark Lover*, Emily Leider, right, signs copies of her new Valentino
biography outside the steps of the Cathedral Mausuleum on August 23, 2003

On your arrival once you climbed the steps to the main entrance of the Cathedral Mausoleum, you found two large wreaths flanking each side of the bronze doors. They were covered in red roses, which was Rudolph's favorite flower. They were held upright on easels. Also the two support columns had greenery foliage roped around them and across the entrance, with a clearance of just six feet, making it appear almost majestic as you walked under, to enter the mausoleum. On the upper part the word "Valentino" was spelled out on the red ribbon, and the word "Forever" on the wreath on the left side of the door. The cemetery spared no expense to honor Rudolph Valentino for yet another year.

Two display cases were lodged in the first two alcove wings down the marble hall that leads to the third alcove, the very one where Rudy is buried. Items displayed from private collections included autographed photos, letters from

Rudy's brother, Alberto, also Mrs. Valentino's favorite recipe as written on Rudolph Valentino's personal stationary in 1924, a movie magazine depicting Valentino on his very first cover appearance, items from the Valentino estate, a rare casting from the original mold of a bust relief done by the famed sculptor, Roger Noble Burnham (who was the sculptor of the *Aspiration* statue.)

At 12:10 p.m., gazing over a packed audience, cemetery owner Tyler Cassity gave the opening remarks, welcoming everyone to the 77th Annual Valentino Memorial. Tyler noted how he was "fascinated" that 77 years after his death, Valentino still had films and books either newly released or currently in production. Cassity then introduced Marc Wanamaker who spoke on the simple fact of "Why Are We Here."

Tyler Cassity gives the opening remarks and welcomes guests to the
Valentino Memorial Service on August 23, 2003

Karie Bible continues the tradition of the Lady In Black. At the 2003 Valentino Memorial she
asks for a brief moment of silence in honor of her predecessors

Then, Tyler introduced the "new" Lady In Black, (Karie Bible) who spoke on the history of the Ladies In Black throughout the years. The speech was almost identical to the one she had delivered last year. Then it was time for the first of the two keynote speakers. The audience warmly welcomed filmmaker and actor Edoardo Ballerini. His remarks were scheduled on "The Importance of Preserving Valentino's Legacy."

Edoardo Ballerini, producer and star of *Goodnight, Valentino* addresses the 77th anniversary
Valentino Memorial Service August 23, 2003

Since Ballerini had portrayed Valentino himself in his short film *Goodnight, Valentino* everyone wanted to hear what he had to say. He acknowledged that this very event was held to honor the Valentino legacy, while pointing out the "irony" that what we were honoring, was in essence the very thing "that made his life difficult." Then he quoted from the famous essay written from noted author H. L. Mencken who had written of a private dinner he had with Valentino in New York just days before Valentino fell ill. Edoardo Ballerini summed it up saying that Valentino "was a man... a man who had troubles like any man."

Tyler Cassity returned to the podium to introduce Jimmy Bangley. Bangley spoke on the talent of Valentino the dancer. He fondly shared his first recollection of his grandmother who told him of her seeing Rudolph Valentino dance in person on the Mineralava Tour in 1923. Jimmy smiled as he told the audience how he could still see the gleam in her eyes when she fondly recalled the occasion. Jimmy also gave a plug to the new book *Dark Lover* and shot a glance at Emily Leider sitting in the guest speaker section saying, "I'm plugging you, lady..."

Anton Gazenbeek and Akiko Baldridge recreate the famous Valentino
tango at the Valentino Memorial Service on August 23, 2003

Next on the lineup was Anton Gazenbeek who, accompanied by Akiko Baldridge would dance the tango to the delight of the audience. They appeared to effortlessly perform the tango dance number made famous by Rudolph Valentino in the *Four Horseman* in 1921.

Emily Leider, author of the newly released and critically acclaimed in-depth biography on Rudolph Valentino entitled *Dark Lover* was the next keynote speaker.

Keynote speaker, Emily Leider discusses her book *Dark Lover* at the 77th anniversary of the Valentino Memorial Service.

She quickly gave a nod of recognition to the tango dancers by opening her remarks with "I can't think of a better way to invoke his spirit, than to perform the tango." Emily then spoke of where her travels had led her, in her quest to unravel the history of Valentino's life. The places included New York, Los Angeles, London, Paris, and last but not least, Valentino's country of origin, Italy. She spoke at length about seeking out and then succeeding in finding the overgrown weeded grave of Bice Guglielmi, Rudy's sister who was born five years prior to his birth, but died three years before he was born. Engraved on the stone was a quotation in both French and Italian, that Leider suggested could also serve as a summing up of Valentino's time on earth: "Her life was like the life of a rose. Just one day." Emily then shifted gears and read a stirring passage from her book telling in detail about the day the Valentino funeral was held in Beverly Hills on September 7, 1926.

Annette Lloyd introduces the video presentation at the 77th Valentino Memorial Service

The next segment of the program was hosted by Annette Lloyd. For the Valentino Memorial Annette oversees and produces a new mini video each year. The video this year was silent and was accompanied by the famous Bob Mitchell at the organ. Interspersed with video footage as well as numerous stills, it served as a reminder yet once more, of the rich legacy Valentino left behind.

For the musical element, Ian Whitcomb, a personality who had a following in the 1960's came to the podium and mentioned that he knew of fame himself, not unlike Valentino's, he said when "both men and women" adored him in his prime.

Regina & Ian Whitcomb sing the 1926 song *There's A New Star In Heaven Tonight*
at the Valentino Memorial Service on August 23, 2003

Ian was accompanied by his wife Regina, as they sang the vintage tune composed in 1926 in Valentino's honor, *There's A New Star In Heaven Tonight.* Ian played his small banjo and was accompanied by Bob Mitchell on the organ. His delivery was so well received that when he asked the audience if they wanted to hear the second verse, it was never in doubt what the answer would be. Reluctant to bequeath the stage just yet, he broke into an unscheduled rendition of *The Sheik of Araby* to the delight of those amused at the impromptu performance. Even after this song had concluded, he danced a quick jig in the isle before finally reclaiming his seat.

To conclude the 77th Anniversary of the Valentino Memorial Services, Tyler then introduced me to the crowd, and mentioned that my book *Valentino Forever* would soon be published. Among my closing remarks I mentioned the significance of this event, that with few exceptions (the Hollywood Bowl's Easter Sunrise Service, and Academy Awards) that the Valentino Memorial Service is the longest continuing annual Hollywood tradition, whose origins date back to 1927. Also, I pointed out the amazing fact that the only motion picture star who has a statue in Hollywood dedicated solely to them, is Rudolph Valentino.

In closing I spoke of my research into the history of the Valentino Memorial Service, emphasizing that I sought the common thread that wove the generations together. It was remembrance. I found that from the conception, almost up until the mid 1960's the Valentino Memorial usually included a reading from the Bible; of the 23rd Psalm. The back side of this years program had that Psalm printed on it, and everyone assembled was invited to join me in reciting it - "out of a continuing of tradition and for remembrance." It was moving to hear everyone's voice raised in unison as the well-known passage of faith was recited.

In 1927, at the conclusion of the first year's memorial, the press openly doubted that there would be any extended interest on the part of the public, past the initial first anniversary. Time has proven them very wrong. The Valentino Memorial Services has evolved from the early stages of deep mourning to today's respectful memorial that is held as a celebration of his life.

I would like to think that Rudolph Valentino would be pleased by the continuous outpouring of affection, past and present, of the many people who's names and deeds fill these pages. Whether as individuals, or as members of a Valentino Guild, their efforts throughout the decades was to keep the flame of remembrance lit for Rudolph Guglielmi Valentino. We here today are living proof of how well they have succeeded.

Epilogue

I am honored that Tracy Terhune asked me to write an epilogue to his history of the annual Valentino Memorial Services in Los Angeles. I've known Tracy for close to ten years and I am aware that this is a subject very close to his heart. In fact, I think he is the perfect person to have taken up the gauntlet and researched this subject so ably, the result of which is this fine book. His dedication to the subject at hand shows in the care he took with this book. Tracy asked me to add my thoughts on the continuing appeal of Rudolph Valentino beyond the year 2000.

To the modern film fan, it is noteworthy that the star that was Rudolph Valentino still shines brightly so many years beyond his untimely death in 1926. To those familiar with his films, his image and his story, the continued appeal is really not so very surprising. The remarkable phenomena of the annual services held for Rudolph Valentino is not only a reflection on the appeal of a star whose life faded before its time, but of a man who represented so much more.

The cult of the Valentino fan has traversed a winding path over the years. In the 1920's, a sense of personal loss and grief were the hallmarks. As time passed, a fond remembrance of a beloved star highlighted the memorials during the dark days of the depression and throughout World War II. After the war, there was a change. A real cult developed and the remembrance became clouded with the resurgence of spiritualism which never truly represented the man himself. While Valentino had a passing interest in spiritualism through his wife, Natacha Rambova, he would have been horrified to have been branded some kind of "saint" to be worshipped. This image was exacerbated by the infighting between the memorial guilds, and continued through the 1950's. In the next two decades, the services continued, the eulogy given by fewer and fewer who knew Valentino the man. But, the fans still came, drawn by some inexorable magic. Valentino's films were scarce, VHS had not been created and only a fervent few attended the film festivals and revivals. Yet Valentino was more of a legend than ever before. The services at this time began to have more than a little bit of a circus atmosphere as the cemetery became a progressively a seedy, run down place. In the 1980's, the services became even greater free for all, yet people came still to pay tribute, younger and younger generations who had no idea what it was like to have seen Valentino in his heyday. In the 1990's, the services were transformed yet again. It was not only the services that survived and prospered, but the cemetery itself. New life breathed into it when the property was saved by the Forever Network. The present owners have a respect for the history of their cemetery and this respect and dignity has since marked the memorial services. The focus, in the modern age, seems to be on memorializing Valentino, the real man, who incidentally happened to be a great star.

With the centenary of Rudolph Valentino's birth in 1995, a window seemed to open and the fresh air coming through fanned the flames of interest in this much-maligned and neglected star. There is a marked difference between the Valentino fan of the 1920's and the Valentino fan of today. While there is little doubt, Rudolph Valentino's appeal on film is still undimmed, it is the truth of the man, the real person behind that sheik image that is the attraction now. Therein lay the difference that would please Rudolph Valentino to no end; people admiring him for his own qualities and recognizing that the image up on the screen was not him.

I attended my first memorial in 1979. It was, in a word, an experience. An afternoon of George Jessel and Estrellita Del Regil made it quite unforgettable! I attended several subsequent memorial services. The one constant was Mary MacLaren along with the die-hard Valentino fans that came year after year. I'm happy to count some of these people, I met then, as friends today. While never a regular attendee of the annual memorials, I can appreciate the feeling of fellowship shared by all who attend regularly. For those who cannot attend, this book provides a terrific history and fills a gap in the mystique of Rudolph Valentino. You can be there without really being there!

Is there a place for Rudolph Valentino beyond the 20th century? Indulge me if I seem biased, but I think the answer to this question is a most emphatic yes. The fan base, while certainly smaller than the throngs of the 1920's, is still fervent and intensely loyal.

The Valentino fan of today is truly blessed. Technology grants us many avenues to seek out information and communicate with one another. They are also afforded a forum to discuss Valentino, his films, and his life via the internet. Generally good natured, sometimes the discussions can become heated as in any chat forum. But the discussion always turns back to the shared subject at hand, a genuine interest in Rudolph Valentino.

For those not connected to the internet (incomprehensible, but true), those fans can keep up with all things Valentino in a printed quarterly newsletter. It is quite surprising the new material and facets or angles about Valentino's life and films that turn up.

New books are being written as more information is discovered. Emily Leider's biography seems to be just the beginning. Riches, indeed!

Additionally, Valentino has been treated fairly in a couple of modern documentaries; The Legend of Rudolph Valentino (available on DVD) and the documentary produced for the A&E Network (and broadcast periodically on A&E and the Biography Channel).

Many of his films are available on DVD. Fans of Valentino, I believe, take for granted how very fortunate they are in this regard. Most of his major starring films still exist and of those, a good number can be viewed easily by the casual film fan. This is another reason his appeal continues, undimmed by time and forgetfulness. Turner Classic Movies holds the rights to the three surviving films he made early in his career, The Four Horsemen of the Apocalypse, The Conquering Power and Camille. TCM shows these films on an annual basis along with regular showings of The Eagle, Blood and Sand and The Son of the Sheik.

Valentino's films are also shown at various film festivals, archives and art houses, thus, further ensuring that there will be new interest in Rudolph Valentino. His face and image in some form or another is still very much before the public.

The collectors among the fan base find daily new treasures on EBay™. The stiff competition for quality and/or unusual items further attests to Rudolph Valentino's continued appeal. From vintage photos and posters and lobby art to reproductions of Valentino's tank watch to mouse pads, t-shirts and light switch covers, there is almost nothing you cannot find that has a likeness of Valentino. Some of the items are cheap and shoddy. Nevertheless, the sales of these items prove there is something about Valentino that makes even the most ridiculous dreck sell.

On a personal level, I host one of the several websites devoted to Rudolph Valentino. Judging by the email I receive from people all over the world, the appeal of Rudolph Valentino is still very potent and magnetic.

For every person, the appeal or magic of Rudolph Valentino is a little bit different. Regardless, of that personal appeal or magic, he will continue to be remembered, his star will never dim and the mystery of his life and death will draw people as moths to a flame. This is a proven fact. Rudolph Valentino would likely be surprised by this. I like to think, in the long run, he would be well pleased to still be a weaver of dreams. For in this day, as in the days of old, his timeless appeal allows people a chance to get away from the stress of daily life and all its troubles. His work and life are viewed today, with one great difference — respect. He would have liked that.

Today, we know Rudolph Valentino was not only an artist; he was a man who well deserves to be remembered for the good works he left behind. *Riposa in pace.*

Donna Hill
December 5, 2003

Introduction to Red Roses At Noon

Our quest to know the person on the other side of the famous black veil, sadly reveals that there is not a lot of information available on Ditra Flame's early or private life. She was born in Wintersburg, California on August 5, 1905, as Ditra Hellena Mefford. Little is known of her early years except for reasons that are unknown today, she was placed for adoption and soon became an embraced member of the Wilson family. The Wilson's already had a daughter close to Ditra's age named Cora. She used the Wilson name, for legal purposes for the rest of her life. In her last years she changed her first and middle name to be called Princess Orvella Wilson. The headstone on her grave has this name on it.

Another mystery is exactly when Ditra began the use of her stage name Ditra Flame. The earliest evidence comes from none other than Rudolph Valentino's business manager, S. George Ullman. In a reply letter dated July 10, 1928, he responds to Ditra Flame, about her submission of a photograph of a man she felt resembled Rudy, in answer to newspaper reports of a motion picture in the works based on the Ullman book *Valentino As I Knew Him.* In a newspaper article in 1929, she again uses Flame as her last name, when discussing a publicity stunt of walking coast-to-coast, from Long Beach California to New York City. In her attempt to lose fifty pounds on the journey, Ditra said "all I am taking with me is my violin." Whether she ever completed this journey is not known. However it's easy to see her hunger for publicity started quite early.

Ditra's story of meeting Valentino in 1919 has been well covered many times in the press, and she made much of her brief friendship with the aspiring Italian actor. When she fell ill a short time later and was in a Pasadena California hospital, Valentino visited her and their pact to visit the grave of whomever died first, was agreed upon at this time. In 1926 when Valentino died in New York, Ditra was 21 years old, living in Oregon.

Ditra claims to have been present, along with thousands of others, at Hollywood Memorial Park Cemetery on September 7, 1926 the day Valentino was buried. After the brief ceremonies in the mausoleum, she witnessed Pola Negri as she exited the bronze doors and collapsed on the front steps.

Over the years Ditra held a variety of jobs. As a young violinist, she worked at the Highland Theatre, which was located just behind the famed Hollywood Hotel. She also ran her own custom dress shop in Banning, called "Sunbonnet Sue's Sewing Shop." Of course she founded and maintained the Valentino Memorial Guild. At the Valentino crypt on August 23, 1954, she declared an end to her annual appearances as The Lady In Black. She proclaimed her faith in God and that her focus would now solely be on missionary work with the Indians. True to her word, Ditra did not return to the Valentino Memorial Services until 1965, and on this visit she dressed in regular attire. She repeated this low-key appearance, and attended again in 1966. She made her last return on August 23,1977 and was, for her final time, dressed in her entire Lady In Black attire.

In interviews Ditra always denied having ever been married. However, court papers provide documentation that in 1930 she was married in Tijuana, Mexico to Gabriel Del Valle. The outcome of this marriage, or of Mr. Del Valle is a mystery. There is no evidence Ditra ever filed for a divorce, and only once did she admit, in writing, to having been married. That revelation was made to author of the famous "Where Are They Now" book series, Richard Lamparski. Unfortunately Ditra didn't go into any details behind the marriage, other than to acknowledge she had indeed been wed.

Ditra lived for several years at 6118 Selma Avenue in Hollywood California. Her house was in the rear, and the front rooms were utilized for her Valentino Memorial Guild offices. Several years later, in the early 1950's in her effort to escape the Los Angeles smog, she moved to Banning, California. Banning is a sleepy city about twenty five miles outside of Palm Springs. She lived quietly there, journeying back to Hollywood each year to attend the Valentino Memorial Services. Seasonally, she also lived on the Indian reservation while she was doing her missionary work. Upon her mother's stroke she put her religious work aside to assist her mother with round the clock nursing care. After her mother's death, Ditra permanently relocated in 1967 to her mother's residence at 613 Vesta Street in Ontario, California. This would become her final home, and as it was here she passed away quietly on February 23, 1984 at the age of 78.

It was a life-long desire of Ditra to have the final say, preferably in the form of her own book. However, she wanted her words to be heard, unedited by reporters playing up old untruths. In her twilight years she began to make written notes for such a project. She also harbored deep fears that someone might make an attempt to sell her book at the Valentino crypt, thus cheapening her Lady In Black title. Should that occur, she penned a vow of disapproval, stating "If this book ever gets in print - and some distributor decides to circulate it at the Valentino tomb – just remember I am not the one who does it. There will be a clause in the contract with the publisher prohibiting such display."

Ditra guarded her claim to the title of the original Lady In Black with a passion and sincerity that of none of her imitators ever managed to equal. However, in a television interview on January 30, 1961 she spoke candidly of what she wanted to happen to the Lady In Black legacy after her departure. Ditra told interviewer Paul Coats in clear terms "I hope really that after I pass on – the tradition of the Lady In Black will be still carried on. I have no jealousy for anyone that would do it in a loving way, and I think Rudy deserves it."

In conclusion, I strongly felt that Ditra deserved to be heard, and so here she is - presented as she wished - unedited. *Red Roses At Noon* was written entirely by her. Nothing has been added, or deleted. Here now, for the first time ever, Ditra Flame has the final say.

Red Roses
at
Noon

By

Ditra Flame

224

Red Roses At Noon

The California sun shines through a stained glass window of the Hollywood Mausoleum magnifying a name beloved by countless people all over the world – Rudolph Valentino. It is now twenty three years since Rudy has left our midst – years fraught with every conceivable happening among men and nations. Yet, for twenty three years the name of Rudolph Valentino has been in print since his death more than any other personage of our time.

There is still overwhelming magic in the name of the young Italian who came to America to find whatever she had to offer him. His reward was hardship, fame and tragedy – then the world. From all parts of the world people come to his crypt to utter one word, "Valentino." Not all who pay homage to him are women, there are just as many men. Today a young Hindu spoke so reverently of him in hushed tones one could almost hear the footsteps of one of his native gods walking in the Shalamar Gardens at Kashmir.

I have heard many a prayer and words of praise at the Valentino tomb. I have seen with my own eyes an elderly Italian patting the bronze plaque that identifies Rudy's crypt, his eyes filled with tears, his voice wrought with emotion crying, "Boy, boy, son of Italy, you be with God now."

A woman, unmistakably his wife, pulled at his sleeve, "Papa, Rodolfo is happy, you be happy too." The old man looked up, his sobs quieted for the moment. "But mama, we so old, he die so young. We dona maka da life happy for people like Rodolfo. Why not God he taka me and leava Rodolfo to bringa da sun?" The woman took his arm and gently guided him away from the crypt and down the corridor.

Abruptly he turned and came shuffling back. He glanced at me for the first time and then shyly looked up to the roses on Rudy's crypt. I told him he could have one since it was I who had placed them there. He thanked me profusely and added, "Lady, I so glad Rodolfo gotta fine friend lika you." When I told him Rudy has many friends even yet, his eyes lighted up with joy and his tenseness relaxed with a sigh. As he turned away it was evident he had found the kind of peace he had hoped to find at Rudy's resting place. This man was sincere, his love for Valentino encircled him. He could have been Rudy's father and so he felt he was.

I have interviewed hundreds of people in the past twenty three years – people who were and are honestly interested and hungry for some bit of information regarding Rudolph Valentino. These people cannot all be neurotics and free lance mystics – nor are they prompted by ulterior motives as supposed by some who believe it to be part of a colossal publicity stunt to keep Valentino's name alive. This idea is impractical because it would take a super colossal fortune to back it up. I think we of the cinema city are prone to cry, "publicity" at the slightest provocation because here even the layman knows that publicity does play an important part in the promotion of those in the artistic professional fields. The general run of people who are still interested in Valentino are non-professionals.

I saw Rudolph Valentino the first time when I was fourteen. He was living in a rooming house at 692 Valencia Street, in Los Angeles. Having spent some time in Mexico I mistook him for a Mexican and started my conversation in Spanish. The illusion was complete because he bubbled forth exuberantly. I felt dreadfully stupid because I lacked a command of the Spanish language and I lost my tongue in embarrassment. He said, "Sorellina, don't feel bad. I could only speak three words of English when I landed in America. I still don't speak well." The barriers were down. The warmth of his understanding made me feel I had known him all my life.

He left a lasting impression upon me which was evident when I was in a Pasadena hospital sometime later. I insisted I had to see Rodolfo Valentino, as he preferred to be called. As I look back now, I know the nurses must have thought me a "movie-struck" child in delirium. But up to that time I had not connected the dark Latin of my first meeting with any personality on the screen.

That night I confided in the intern who had previously observed me kindly and he produced the pencil and paper upon which I wrote a note to Rudy, and he mailed it. The expression on the nurse's face was worth all my persistence when three days later, Valentino actually appeared at the hospital and entered my room.

"What are you doing here, Sorellina?" he exclaimed. "I have an abscess in my ear and the doctor thinks I will have to be operated upon," I replied tearfully. "No, no! That must not be!" He excitedly paced the floor. "But I feel terrible!" I insisted. I must admit I wasn't lying. The pain was excruciating. In fact, I was so certain I was not long for this world that I bluntly told him so.

Instead of laughing at me or saying anything trite in an attempt to raise my spirits, he became very serious. "I do not think it is time for you to die, Sorellina. But if you do, you will not be lonely because I will come every day to talk to you. Everything will be fine. I will bring you flowers and other people will too." "If there will be so many flowers how will I know which ones are from you?" I asked in all earnestness. "Because my flowers will be different from the others. You will know. I will bring you a whole bunch of oleanders. Remember, Sorellina?"

Then he said something that was imprinted upon my mind for the remainder of my life. "If I die before you do, I will expect something from you." "Oh, yes, anything," I cried, hoping to please him. "What will it be?"

"Very little, but it will mean very much to me. Just one red rose. Is it a promise?" I promised, and that moment I decided to live. His philosophy had worked the miracle because he had talked to me about what had been worrying me and made it seem all right.

Every time I saw him after that, he was usually racing off to the various appointments that make up the daily round of the movie colony. He rushed through life as though he were crowding a hundred years into a few short hours.

But he gleaned more from his thirty one years than most people do who live to a ripe old age.

After a rapid conversation which was usually one sided because I wanted to hear all about his news, he would rush out of the house to his car, leap into it as though mounting a fiery steed and take off like a streak of lightning, never forgetting to raise his arm in a debonair gesture, "goodbye for now." When his car disappeared from sight I invariably stood transfixed by his forceful personality. He was all personality. This was his greatest asset, the seed for his ultimate triumph in pictures. For such a personality to lack egotism is most unusual but I have never seen him attempt to impress anyone that he knew all the answers. He was too busy trying to improve himself. I couldn't see for the life of me how anyone with his naturally dramatic, unaffected individuality could ever hope for improvement. I am not trying to place a halo around Rudy's dark, lustrous head, nor am I saying he was above the moodiness, impulsiveness and passions of the human race. However, he was one of those rare mortals who made more than an attempt at perfection.

I can truthfully say that few people ever understood Rudolph Valentino, and perhaps this was one of his mysterious attractions. In fact, I have heard him say, "I do not understand myself. If I could I would know where I am going. There seems to be a dark shade that I cannot penetrate." Little did he or anyone know at he time that the dark shade which his sensitive mind actually sensed was the shadow of the Valley of Death. This subconscious uncertainty which marked his life was responsible for his feeling of utter loneliness. At times one could catch a glimpse in his eyes of remote horizons. Apparently merged with the skies he would say, "There are so many worlds out there...so many." It was as though he was trying to reach out in search of his destination. Then he would continue by saying, "but few people live rightly in this one. We can have majestic thoughts in a hermit's hut, or we can think as a swine in a palace. All we have to do is choose our station. Eternity is the Empire." This was the part of his nature that expanded beyond this realm of material existence.

Rudy feared nothing in life nor did he fear the realms of the departed. In fact, he did not consider the departed anything but people without the bonds of flesh. However, there was a certain instinct within him that made him shy away from things not of this earth. Not because he was afraid but because he felt that in some mysterious way his life was linked up with something over and beyond... something he could not altogether comprehend, though glimpsed in a moment of reflection. Little did he realize that it was moments like these which helped him to surmount his greatest difficulties – the parting with a loved one, and death itself.

Love was the most important factor in his life and the irony was that he could never hold it in his grasp. The perfect love which he so ardently desired produced the perfect manifestation of love on the screen. Any woman living under the same roof with Rudolph Valentino would have to have to have had more than a woman's intuition. It would have required a profound occult nature reflecting his every mood to have complied with his startling expectations.

Above all of Rudy's attributes I admired his honesty. He never hid his emotions under the guise of pretense. He was too frank to have concealed motives. He usually did exactly as he felt at the moment, sometimes to his regret. "Things have a way of shaping up but I can't seem to wait for that. My impatience is my undoing." But discouraging thing that were said to him and that were printed about him did not adjust themselves so easily. These were deep jagged scars which I and others know he carried to his grave, and perhaps beyond. He was extremely sensitive and could never forget disappointments or unjust criticism. People hurt him more than they will ever know.

The word 'sheik' as applied to a sleek haired Latin lover was most distasteful to him. The 'pink powder puff' editorial printed in a Chicago paper shortly before his death was an attempt to defame his masculinity. To say that it merely hurt his pride is putting it mildly. Anyone who saw his agonized expression, his jaw set firmly, the muscles of his face drawn taunt, muttering in a throated whisper, "Swine! How could they print such stuff!" would know that the thrust of slander

229

had reached his core. His deeply felt emotion was as much in defense of the reading public as it was in the defense of himself. He was intensely masculine through he wore a slave bracelet which he dared anyone to remove.

For the past twenty three years Valentino's name has been in print under every conceivable heading. I quote a few: "Tragic Valentino" –"Valentino Estate Auctioned" – "Ex-Wife Tells Valentino Spirit Message" –"Valentino Houses Haunted" –"Valentino's Loves Revealed" – Then there were the more sorted by-lines: "Woman Commits Suicide At Valentino Memorial" –"Occult Forgery Directed By Valentino's Spirit" – "Love Trysts Kept At Valentino's Grave By Love Starved Women."

The Lady in Black headline went beyond the wildest dreams of Russell Birdwell, a former newspaper reporter, who claims to have created it, the reason for which is still remote. Perhaps he had previously heard rumors of a real 'Lady in Black', and was alerted to a sensational story.

Pola Negri was the first woman to wear black at Valentino's tomb. Over a black dress she wore a black draped coat, a black turban with a long black veil. I saw her collapse on the steps of the Hollywood mausoleum in September 1926. Her grief was unmistakable. I have worn the Lady in Black attire to Rudy's tomb for twenty three years to keep my promise to him.

There have been others who, for various reasons, have posed as the Lady in Black. Rouben Mamoulian wanted the original mystery woman to play an anonymous role in 'Blood and Sand', a re-make of the Valentino picture. He inserted an ad in the papers for the woman, and no less than seventeen impostors showed up. They were recognized as impostors because the real Lady in Black was known to be middle aged, heavy set, and tall. The 'would be' candidates were of chorus girl measurements. Obviously they were trying anything to get a chance in pictures.

An ex-follies girl claims she is the real Lady in Black and insists she has the right to the throne because she gave birth to two of Valentino's children. She has never been able to prove her claims, and she has since been committed to a sanitarium by the courts as 'irrational.'

There have been others who have claimed Valentino to be the father of their children. Mr. S. George Ullman, Rudy's business manager for several years, informed me that at the time of Rudy's death no less than two hundred letters were received making claims to his parenthood, many of them from married women.

Memorial day of this year, when the Hollywood Rudolph Valentino Memorial Guild placed flowers at his crypt, we found a floral offering with a card reading, "From Your Beloved Son." The card was quickly removed from the prying eyes of the onlookers. We tried to trace the sender but there was no address on record at the florist. The flowers had been wired from Detroit, Michigan. I felt that if I could talk with the person who had sent the flowers I might be instrumental in bringing him closer to the real Valentino and in some way relieve any conflict that he may have been laboring under.

I have a treasured picture of Rudy with Mr. Ullman's children. He adored them. He hoped that one day he would have a large, rollicking family, so characteristic of all Italians. To show his idealistic thoughts of all children I quote from his book 'Day Dreams': "A baby's skin – texture of a butterfly's wing, colored like a dawned rose, whose perfume is the breath of God. Such is the web wherein is held the treasure of the treasure chest, the priceless gift – the child of love." Anyone who loved children as did he, would never have given up any child whose birth he was responsible for. He never realized his dream of fatherhood and more is the pity.

Many who saw Valentino's all consuming personality on the screen or elsewhere, were so possessed with it that he became their living companion. They felt that in some mysterious way he was related to them. I believe this bond is what has given rise in many instances to the claims made upon him.

Recently I received a letter from a young man in Yorkshire, England. He writes, "I have for some time been engaged in collecting information dealing with the late Rudolph Valentino, who's famous career incidentally, I am too young to have witnessed, but in whom I have had an interest amounting to fascination. As a man this might seem a little odd, save that even now, I can recognize that Valentino was a very fine actor. His picture, 'The Eagle' is currently playing at London's Cameo Cinema." This is only one of the many letters from the younger generation showing its response to the Valentino appeal, though his pictures were filmed over twenty three years ago. This apparent demand for Valentino pictures has stimulated a competitive race between Jan Grippo of Monogram Studios who will film the 'Return of Valentino', and Edward Small whose production will be 'The Life of Valentino.'

There have been many legends woven around the colorful personality of Rudolph Valentino. Among the more prominent Is the story of a 'Valentino Jinx'. The seed of this jinx story was sown by Rudy himself when he said of his first picture, "The picture is jinxed. I got off to a bad start." The picture tied up by a lien was later released as 'The Married Virgin.' Since this was Rudy's first part (before this he had been an extra) I doubt if he ever quite got over the idea that he was dogged by ill fate, the contrast of which was his implicit belief in 'kismet'. He knew he would ultimately become successful in pictures.

I have known only one person who actually believed in a 'Valentino jinx.' In 1925 Valentino consented to pose for a well known Italian sculptor. After the bust was finished, Rudy wanted some changes made and this the sculptor vehemently refused to do. An argument ensued and Rudy stalked out of the studio.

Several years later, while I was studying with the same sculptor, I discovered the statue covered with a canvas and I insisted upon bringing it out of hiding. He reluctantly consented. For several weeks it was apparent that his resentment toward the statue was smoldering. One afternoon I entered the studio just in time to see that resentment kindled into inflamed fury. He was attempting to destroy my treasured object with an ax. When I asked him why he wanted to destroy such a beautiful piece of art, he screamed, "Mr. Valentino, he no like my work! My business bad. He curse me. I hid him for years, now I have to see him again. I see him in my sleep. I fix him so no one see him again!" I told the raging sculptor I was deeply sorry if I was in any way responsible for bringing Valentino back into his life. I informed him that if he would bury the statue for posterity, instead of destroying it, I would promptly bring my sculpturing career to a close. Some time later I heard he had suddenly passed away. Fortunately, I had previously obtained a picture of the only statue of Valentino for which he had actually posed.

Shortly after Rudy's death the story that his houses were haunted grew like wildfire. An air of sanctity enveloped them which non-plussed the real estate men. No one wanted the Valentino homes—Falcon Lair in Beverly Hills and the Valentino Villa in Hollywood. These stories were the result of the suddenness of his death. It was as though the houses still belonged to him. He had gone away only for a little while and would return. Return he did not, and the places were eventually sold. They changed hands several times, each of the occupants claiming an aura of restlessness surrounded the places which was attributed to Rudy's ghost. In centuries to come, if Hollywood ever becomes another Theban ruins, posterity will surely discover other legends about the miraculous Rudolph Valentino.

Rudy hated macabre publicity and I dare not think what his attitude would be if he could voice his opinion on the current story in print — "Was Valentino Murdered?" I can imagine his dark eyes flashing in anger and narrowing in contempt, saying, "death is not even sacred and all for the sake of a story!"

I feel the deepest sympathy for those who attended at his bedside, keeping constant vigil during the last hours of his fatal illness, who even yet, can feel the sting of this experience. Also, for his friends who are now horror struck at the possibility that their beloved Rudy may have been sent to an early grave by the hand of a ruthless murderer.

Mr. George Ullman was with him through his last illness. Who better could know the nature of that illness? I realized that to speak to Mr. Ullman about Rudy's death was like opening an old wound because he was, and still is, one of Valentino's sincerest friends. He said, "there is not one word of truth in the current story that Rudy met with foul play. I was with him when he was stricken. Why don't these people try to verify the facts before making insinuations? Anyone who saw Rudy's once rugged body wasted by the effects of disease could never doubt for one moment that his death could be attributed to anything other than natural causes." Rudy was actually ailing several weeks before his collapse after a party given in the apartment of Barclay K. Warburton Jr.

Those at Rudy's bedside other than Mr. Ullman were Father Leonard who administered the last rites of the Roman Catholic Church and a few minutes before death he held a crucifix to Valentino's lips as he passed on, murmuring incoherent Italian. Joseph Schenck of United Artists Picture Corporation and the attending physicians were also present.

There were five doctors on the case. Four attending physicians, Dr. Harold Meeker who had performed surgery on Valentino, Doctors Durham and Denning, and Dr. William Bryant Rawless, the Polyclinic Hospital physician, and Dr. Eugene Poole, a New York specialist. The following statement was made by the doctors at the time of death:

"Mr. Valentino was overwhelmed with septis, which means he died of poisoning. He died of septic endo-carditis, a poisoning of the cardiac nerves of the heart. His stomach was perforated and flood passed into the abdominal cavity which resulted in the poisoning."

Rudolph Valentino was operated on under date of August 15th, 1926 at Polyclinic Hospital, New York, for gastric ulcers and acute appendicitis. August 16th he suffered from peritonitis. August 21st he took a turn for the worse developing pleurisy. August 22nd his temperature was 104 and he died the following day, at noon. Alberto Guglielmi (Valentino's brother) evidently overcome by his brother's death, perhaps felt that everything had not been done that could have been done. Unable to speak but little English he went to an Italian doctor in Brooklyn. The doctor, after listening to Alberto's story, went to the District Attorney of New York and made certain accusations which the District Attorney found to have no basis.

I hope these statements will forever still the suspicions and fears of anyone who imagines Rudolph Valentino died of foul play. The records speak for themselves.

There are many people in whose lives Valentino is still an inspiration. One young man who is struggling in the motion picture field tells me that when he becomes downhearted, all he has to do is to think of Rudy without friends or a job during his first days in New York, too broke to pay for a two dollar a week room. Others lay their success to the generosity of Valentino, and a few claim their very lives have been spared because of him. In England and America, societies have long been organized to perpetuate his memory by benevolent activities. Each Christmas, gifts are taken to an Italian hospital in London. There is the 'Valentino Ward for Children', which is available to children of all nationalities.

In the future there will be a lovely wedding chapel gracing the hills of Hollywood designed after a chapel in Castellaneta, Italy, Rudy's birthplace. It is to be a living memorial to Rudolph Valentino and dedicated to lovers all over the world. It will be sponsored by the members of the Hollywood Rudolph Valentino Memorial Guild.

Many personages of great note have passed on and it was an accepted fact, but Valentino's death stunned the world and it refused to believe it. Thousands of people waited hours in drenching rain to view for the last time, the classical features of their 'beloved.' The late Arthur Brisbane said of Valentino, "no death since that of Abraham Lincoln has caused the excitement produced by the death of this great film star."

Time proves the immortality of man, at least so far as this world is concerned. When the memory of those who have passed on, become stronger in our mind and in our hearts we know life holds more treasures than we can account for and that even death has it's reward.

The mysterious element of immortality is something far beyond the accomplishments of the human brain and the creations of human hands. It is a breathing, vital spirit that is left indelibly imprinted on that subtle quality within us which we call the soul. The world refuses to believe Valentino dead because it is impossible to associate the state of death with so vibrant a spirit. He lives and endures because he possessed that rare quality capable of touching the soul. This placed him first in the Hall of Fame, then transplanted him to the Garden of Remembrance, and now, to the endless realms of the Immortals.

The shadows lengthen in the marble corridor of the mausoleum. The caretaker motions that it is time for us to leave... The people hesitate to take one more swift glance at the bronze plaque, RUDOLFO GUGLIELMI VALENTINO 1895-1926. Slowly, they walk to the huge bronze doors and silently depart.

I hesitate on the marble steps... a warm desert breeze envelops me... the scent of oleanders fills the air. Standing before me is a boyish young man, friendly, smiling... his dark eyes luminous, kind. "Sorellina,"... he whispers... "they have not forgotten me."

Rudy on the Web

These websites are designed to assist you in your quest to find factual, informative places to visit on the web that pertain to Rudolph Valentino. Access to all of the sites is free of charge. The benefits of each site is indicated

Valentino Forever - This newly conceived website is designed to be the web counterpart to this book. It is my hope to include more photos, documents and also to update future Valentino Memorial Service information as it happens. A continuing work in progress! The web URL is: **www.valentinoforever.com**

"We Never Forget" - Valentino Yahoo e-group - allows interaction via daily posts, with other Valentino enthusiasts. In operation since 2000, this popular group functions as the host for almost 200 people who all share a common interest in discussing new Valentino projects, or even discussing common Valentino topics. All are welcome to join, and it's free of charge. The web URL is: **http://groups.yahoo.com/group/Rudolph_Valentino/**

Rudolph Valentino Newsletter - Back by popular demand, this newsletter is a must for those who want to be kept up to date on all things Valentino. Full of rare photos, articles by noted Valentino authorities, the Valentino Newsletter is something that no real Valentino fan would find themselves without. For subscription information the web URL is:
http://www.rudolph-valentino.com/newsletter.htm

Rudolph Valentino Homepage - Often called the best Valentino website, and for good reason. It's impossible to find a superior place on the internet pertaining to Valentino, than the "Rudolph Valentino Homepage." Packed with photos, articles, examples of Valentino signatures, even a "tour" through Valentino's home, Falcon Lair. Valentino updates, including new book, film, and DVD releases is provided. There is always the eagerly anticipated poster of the month to keep you returning. To visit this Valentino site the URL is: **http://www.rudolph-valentino.com**

Printed in the United States
26015LVS00001B/129-168